DESIGN AWARENESS

DESIGN AWARENESS

ROBERT SOMMER

Chairman, Department of Psychology
University of California
Davis, California

RINEHART PRESS

San Francisco

© 1972 by Rinehart Press
5643 Paradise Drive
Corte Madera, Calif. 94925

A division of Holt, Rinehart and Winston, Inc.

Library of Congress Catalog Number: 77-179628

03-080298-9

Printed in the United States of America

2 3 4 5   038   9 8 7 6 5 4 3 2 1

To Barbara

Preface

People want a voice in the design and use of their buildings, streets, parks, and cities. They want to be more than spectators and consumers in a world designed and managed by remote professionals. They want to be more than passengers on a spaceship; they want to help design and personalize their cabins and passageways and to have a go at the controls. Yet it is not enough to give people options. They must know how to use them and also the consequences of exercising them. There is no point in making people aware of their environment if they have no way of influencing it. Participation without awareness produces ignorance and ugliness; awareness without participation leads to frustration and alienation.

The first half of this book deals with people who use buildings (environmental consumers) and their role in decisions about the design and management of their immediate environment. We will be discussing environment not as something abstract and distant, but rather in terms of the homes, offices, and communities in which people live, work, and play. Emphasis will be on methods of developing environmental awareness and on the consequences of this awareness in regard to user-generated and user-maintained systems. More specifically, we will be concerned with the relationship between the people who design and manage spaces and those who use them. Similar sorts of questions about the social effects of design appear at every scale of environmental planning, from the interior designer who seeks to learn the proper sorts of furnishings for tenants in public housing to the Army Corps of Engineers who want to know how they can find "what the public wants" so they can provide it.

The second half of this book discusses methods of evaluating existing designs and ways to use this information to find new and better ones. An occasional mismatch between building and occupants is tolerable; the present situation of successive replications of bad solutions certainly is not. The feedback process from existing structures must be developed and institutionalized—no design should exist without evaluation, no evaluation without redesign.

I have benefited greatly from discussions with design students and faculty members thoughout the country. There is a new design culture intensely concerned with user involvement in environmental decision-making. If I have not been able to answer all of the questions I have been asked, I hope that this book will at least state some of the questions in such a way that answers can be generated from the very bright and perceptive people who originally asked the questions.

I owe many ideas to Humphrey Osmond, Sim van der Ryn, and Philip Thiel. Natalie Gumas was kind enough to make her file on People's Park available to me. Nancy Russo read the original manuscript and made many helpful comments. Margaret Hill has been both a good friend and a good secretary. Portions of the chapter on People's Art appeared originally in *Natural History* magazine.

Davis, California

ROBERT SOMMER

Contents

PART ONE: SOCIAL DESIGN

PART TWO: EVALUATION

DESIGN
AWARENESS

PART ONE

Social Design

CHAPTER ONE

The New Designers

Let a Thousand Parks Bloom

Breaking the stillness of a May evening in 1969, bulldozers leveled several small lots in Berkeley, California. Repercussions were heard around the world. In the resulting furor one young man died, two were permanently injured, 482 people were arrested, and court cases still continue. Living in California, I find it difficult to realize that people in other parts of the country may not remember People's Park. I have discovered that even college freshmen in this state may not have heard of it. Since time is moving more rapidly than ever before, it may be helpful if I present a brief chronicle of events.

The park story begins with a small piece of land a few blocks from the Berkeley campus. Several modest residences had been built there. In 1967 the University of California administration perceived that the character of the surrounding neighborhood was deteriorating, and, despite protests from the community, purchased the land for one and three-tenths million dollars and tore down the houses. The University had no immediate plans to build in the area, and the vacant land became an untended parking lot, full of pot holes, old beer cans, and weeds.

By spring of 1969, the street culture in Berkeley was becoming increasingly vocal and militant. Its ranks had been swelled by young people who had come into the San Francisco Bay Area for the "Summer of Love" and remained. The street people were developing a spectrum of neighborhood institutions which emphasized participation, sharing, impulse expression, and the expansion of consciousness. Out of this came Switchboard, a community telephone information service, and the Free Store, where used clothing was collected and given away, free clinics, communes, underground papers, and other things that seemed new at the time. Almost everything had its counterpart in other places or at other times, but in 1969 they seemed to fit together into a particular life style.

As summer approached, the Berkeley street people became concerned with the deteriorating physical environment around Telegraph Avenue. The same creative impulses that had gone into the free clinic and the free church began to focus on the vacant litter-strewn lots in the area. People asked why these vacant lots could not become parks—not the typical manicured lawns and neat rows of trees that are maintained by the city, but different kinds of parks created and maintained by the neighborhood itself. Leaflets and notices in underground papers announced that park development activities would begin on April 20. Many people from the surrounding area, including mothers with children and retired people who wanted to plant something with their own hands, joined in the activity. It has been estimated that almost one thousand people a day were involved in this project. Design students as well as professional landscape designers and architects in the area contributed labor, expertise, and equipment for bringing in soil and planting shrubs and trees. Governor Ronald Reagan viewed this activity as a threat to law and order and so did several members of the University Board of Regents. Although the students voted overwhelmingly to keep the land as a park, their votes could not eradicate the powerful pressures upon the Chancellor of the University of California to reclaim the land. At 3 A.M. on May 14, 1969, University employees and Berkeley police posted "No Trespassing" signs around the park. Early the following morning, police moved in with rifles and tear gas, and an 8 foot high wire mesh fence was constructed around the site. Several days of disturbances ensued involving students, street people, police and National Guardsmen.[1]

The noise has subsided now. Several other user-generated parks that sprang up later in other places are still operating, but the original People's Park has again become a parking lot. It is paved now, still surrounded by the high wire mesh fence, and it is patrolled by security guards. Yet this small plot of ground and the memory of those few weeks of development by neighborhood people provide a landmark in recent architectural history. Environmentalist Alan Temko[2] described it as "the most significant innova-

---

[1]A more detailed chronology of events is presented in Alan Copeland, ed., *People's Park*. New York: Ballantine Books, Inc., 1969.

[2]Alan Temko, "People's Park Needs Help," leaflet distributed by People's Park developers, May 14, 1969.

tion in recreational design since the great public parks of the 19th and 20th Century." Architect Sim van der Ryn[3] called it the forerunner of a new kind of environmental planning which would follow up user-generated design with community control. Syndicated columnists referred to the park as the first conscious stirrings of the ecology activists. Both the revolutionary who dreamed of mass action and the conservative who lived in fear of it were concerned with what they considered illegal seizure of private property. For design professionals as well as for environmental consumers, there was a second issue at stake with far-reaching consequences. As Temko and van der Ryn point out, the idea of people designing and maintaining their own surroundings implies fundamental changes in the role of the designer and in the nature of the client. Instead of a well-to-do patron or a corporate board the client consists of incohesive groups of people who intend to use the facilities.

This new design culture does not rely on self-conscious novelty nor even on the traditional design values of cohesiveness, integrity, perceptual clarity, and loyalty to materials. Without rejecting the latter, the new culture has added a superordinate value—suitability to the needs of the user. Good designers have always been aware of the client's needs. The increasing complexity of society has produced so many nonuser clients, such as corporate boards and government agencies, that the humane designer needs to go beyond the client's prescription in order to discover the needs of the actual users. This concern is not new, but within the last decade it has become a self-conscious ideological movement within the design profession. The new environmentalist sees himself as an architect, landscape designer, or interior decorator not only in the sense of technical competence. He extends his operational base and philosophical justification to the people whose lives will be affected by his decisions. Some of these men and women entirely reject narrow professional labels and would like to call themselves environmentalists or human ecologists. The label is less important than the social role and its performance by the professional.

Changes will occur in the format and content of building programs as soon as these new architects begin writing them. Designers who are concerned with user behavior are likely to write programs that can be evaluated in these terms. It will not be an easy goal to realize. Sociological jargon can be just as vague and ambiguous as architectural jargon. Yet we are going to see more plans in which the programs are written in terms that can be proved or disproved. In the past, architectural programs were often merely public relations documents. Since there was no feedback on projects after they were in use this seemed to be sufficient. In the final analysis it is not the program statement which is most relevant, nor the success or failure of

[3]S. van der Ryn, "Concepts of Space and the Environment." Unpublished manuscript.

the architect in realizing his goals, but rather the methods for generating valid and shareable design information from completed projects.

The danger exists that these social concerns of the new designers will become only another fad—artistic intuition will be replaced by altruistic intuition. In each case the designer believes he knows how other people should live, but the standards of judgment shift from the aesthetic to the sociological. A recent article about Swedish architecture laments that students are now "sociologists first and architects second," and attempt to "use their future profession to serve their ideology."[4] Commenting upon this report in a personal communication, Humphrey Osmond stated that the architect as a social engineer is probably no more satisfactory than the architect as a sculptor, or as a "philosopher king." He suggested that architects might start out as zoo designers do, and take a rather close look at the animal for which they are designing. The optimal conditions for so variable a creature as man, especially when his strength as a species lies in this variability, involve the provision of a wide range of choices. The architect's task is to design in such a way that the individual's choices can be met and not to impose his own choices on others.

There can be no dichotomy between good design and usable design or between beauty and function in architecture. To look beyond the physical structure of a building to its social consequences, to the sorts of people and activity it will contain, and to its effect upon the surrounding community is a necessary aspect of good design. Whether the result will receive top rating according to the classical standards of beauty, regularity, and symmetry is another matter. The new designer tends to side-step this question. As demonstrated in People's Park, the design values lean toward excitement, spontaneity, flexibility, and participation. One can contrast the scruffy and chaotic design of People's Park with the regularity, straight lines, and well-manicured appearance of most city parks. However, the new designer would insist that both parks be considered *with the users in them*, and in the context of their role in neighborhood life.

At one time a professional man could retain his innocence all the way through graduate school. The young apprentice could enter his field indoctrinated with notions of excitement, beauty, and timelessness. These emotions were necessary for recruiting young people into various professions and for supplying the motive force for them to endure the arduous training and apprenticeship periods. Afterward, when it was time to start practice, professional disillusionment would arrive. No longer would the young doctor have access to a full spectrum of medical services—he might have to practice medicine in a small town with an inadequate hospital and an

[4]Roland Huntford, "In Sweden, They Are Sociologists First, Architects Second," Washington *Post*, July 26, 1970, p. H6.

inept pharmacist. The law graduate found that his practice might involve politics, bribery, drudgery, and apprenticeship in a mediocre firm. The young architect faced a drafting board in the back row of a city office where he could work for years creating stereotyped buildings before he might be allowed to design a single building from start to finish.

The time for such disillusionment has been moved forward. Today a greater sophistication concerning the nature of society and of the role of technical experts exists in graduate and professional schools. The young scientist is still concerned with techniques of research and discovery, but he knows that there are superordinate needs—learning who chooses his research problems and discovering to what use his findings will be put. Design students no longer merely ask technical questions about construction methods or philosophical questions about the nature of beauty. Their most important questions turn out to be related to finding out who determines what is built, where it is built, who gets dispossessed by it, and how the effect of a building on its occupants and neighborhood can be measured. No one is able to practice his profession today and be oblivious to the rest of society. There is nothing wrong with helping clients with legal problems or with healing sick bodies, but there is more to the professional person's responsibility. He is obliged to ask whether all segments of society, including people in the slums and Appalachia, sex deviants and drug addicts, the elderly and the infirm, have sufficient access to professional services. At the present time the answer is obviously negative. Often the availability of professional services is inversely proportionate to the need for such services. This paradox is nowhere clearer than in the field of architecture. People who live in slums and in run-down housing developments have the greatest need for design services and have the least access to them. Only the well-to-do person or corporate or governmental clients are able to hire their own architects.

Buckminster Fuller in his *Operating Manual for Spaceship Earth*[5] suggests directing all efforts into cleaning up the ship and getting it to work properly rather than into trying to reform the passengers. Fuller assumes that when individual needs are met, conflicts and discords between groups will cease. His manual spells out what has to be done if we are to provide suitable accommodations for all passengers. Although the model is intellectually challenging and aesthetically attractive, it is deficient in psychological attributes. Even when the material needs of earth's passengers are satisfied, it will not necessarily make them happy or creative. Serious problems exist in the suburbs as well as in the slums, in the cities as well as on the farms. The problems are different, but there is no possibility of equating material

[5]Buckminster Fuller, *Operating Manual for Spaceship Earth*. Carbondale: Southern Illinois University Press, 1969.

success with personal satisfaction. In addition to an operating manual for the spaceship, we need user manuals for individual cabins, storage closets, passageways, and rooms. Education must concern itself with the microcosm of people in their immediate environments; this is where the quality of life must ultimately be measured.

Nor is it enough to provide amenities aboard the spaceship without knowing whether the passengers really want them or know how to use them. Technically it would be possible to cram another five million people onto Manhattan Island, but it is not necessarily desirable. The key issue concerns environmental quality, to which we are clinging more tenaciously since other values have been scattered by secular winds. The phrase *environmental quality* will lose its meaning and become a rhetorical husk, if we cannot define its components, which include meaningful education, decent housing, productive leisure activities, and creative vocations. In his book *The Yoga and the Commissar*, Arthur Koestler[6] makes a distinction between those who want to change man from within through meditation, education, and self-discipline, and those who want to change him from without by creating the proper sort of living and working conditions. These are two contrasting approaches to perfecting the human species; either one by itself is not enough. An unwholesome environment will blemish the finest character structure or might eliminate the entire human species; on the other hand, passive, uncreative individuals will not be able to accomplish much even in the best of environments. Temporary gains can result from either strategy, but the most successful approach involves combining them both—developing institutions and policies which will encourage active, creative, and aware human beings as well as designing environments which will respond to the inputs of those who live in them. A man needs to make changes in his own surroundings and needs to create and express himself. It is not enough for him to be merely a consumer, a spectator, or a passenger.

In an era of rapid technological changes, designers know less and less about the ways in which their products and solutions will be used. Serge Boutourline[7] believes that the work of a physical designer must be supplemented by that of the *environmental manager*, a person who helps individuals or organizations maximize the utilization of existing environments. Whether or not an environmental action is labeled "management" rather than "design" depends upon when the decision is made and how long its outcome is expected to endure. The manager's decisions are reversible, they affect the immediate environment of a specific population of users following

[6]Arthur Koestler, *The Yoga and The Commissar and Other Essays*. New York: The Macmillan Company, 1965.

[7]Serge Boutourline, "The Concept of Environmental Management," *Dot Zero*, IV, September, 1967.

the action, and they are made within the context of the existing social-physical system. The environmental manager compensates for his lack of power to make structural alterations with his greater knowledge of the total system, including the people involved in it. Many creative roles for designers who wish to help people get the most from their surroundings exist in the space management field. For example, we need engineers and others to design new and better automobiles; we also need repairmen and travel consultants who will help car owners get the best use out of their present vehicles.

The New Consumers

From the standpoint of the design professions, there were two different issues involved in People's Park. The first was user-generated design or the involvement of people in creating the kind of spaces they wanted. The second was the insistence of the developers upon community control of the user-designed spaces. Designers have not faced the implications of planned environments which are maintained by the occupants. They doubt that users know enough or care enough to maintain their own community institutions. However, it is no longer possible to overlook the emergence of a new environmental consumer who wants to have some control over his surroundings. In organizations like the Sierra Club and Active Conservation Tactics one sees the emergence of a consumer movement concerned with large scale environmental problems. This development has been assisted by the advocate roles in the design and planning professions. The new consumers, including technical persons as well as laymen, are better educated and have access to a tremendous amount of information. This increases their dismay at their inability to share in decision-making roles. The policies of government agencies tend to be producer-oriented, while universities seem detached from consumer issues. The new consumer's inputs at the polls or in letters to his newspaper or congressman are too miniscule to have much effect. This results in the individual's alienation, powerlessness, and detachment from environmental issues. A free-market analogy breaks down when it comes to public services such as roads, schools, hospitals, housing projects, and other public buildings. Rather than participate in a token manner, the consumer withdraws to a smaller and more comprehensible reality. His apartment or his home, his neighborhood, and his local institutions take on an increased significance. He would like some decision-making role at least at this comprehensible level. There is a clear need for techniques to increase environmental awareness of a person's immediate surroundings.

Most remote from the consumer are those decisions made at the national and state levels. Doxiadis[8] believes that the major dimensions of the earth are shrinking while the minor ones are expanding. When attempting to solve global problems, one must not lose sight of the most important planning module—the individual and his immediate environment. The designer's role requires providing inputs for the consumer at this scale. This may mean bringing the residents of a housing project together to discuss maintenance problems or neighborhood improvements. It may mean undertaking the necessary research to present the pros and cons of different sorts of housing to the elderly. The task will be immeasurably easier if a data bank on existing facilities exists. Once the community has agreed on what it wants, the designer's task is to help bring the plans into realization as a three-dimensional form which allows for changing needs and circumstances.

The street people who developed People's Park in Berkeley, like the participants in the Woodstock Rock Festival, were proud of the fact that they policed themselves. Although it is difficult to get unbiased accounts of events, the developers of the first People's Park maintained that there were no robberies or violence there and that this was a direct result of community identification with the park. In many institutions of the counterculture, a desire for this sort of self-maintenance exists. This type of system broke down, however, at the Altamont Rock Festival where the managers appointed a motorcycle gang (the Hell's Angels) as policemen instead of relying on the total community, and the results included numerous beatings and at least one violent death attributable to the appointed "policemen."

Professor C. T. Sorenson, who pioneered the adventure playground in Denmark, states clearly that some kind of adult supervision is necessary.[9] But although an adult leader may be necessary, his role is different from what it is in a conventional playground. He is considered a helper, gives assistance when asked, and refrains from offering it gratuitously. He is responsible for helping the children to develop a system to keep track of tools. He qualifies as an advocate professional (or nonprofessional) in the sense that he helps the children accomplish what they wish; he is not there to organize activities that cater to adult prejudices.

Although the number of major incidents of violence against people or property was small at both People's Park and Woodstock, there were significant problems regarding health and sanitation facilities and the nuisance to other persons in the vicinity. The promoter of the Altamont festival was later sued by local ranchers for damage done to their property. The devel-

[8]C. A. Doxiadis, "Man and the Space Around Him," *Saturday Review,* December 14, 1968, pp. 21–23.

[9]H. B. Olsen, "Environments for Creative Play," *Proceedings of the 1969 Park and Recreation Administrators Institute.* Davis, California: University Extension, University of California, Davis, 1970.

opers of People's Park were conscious of these issues and tried to obtain self-adherence to an unwritten code of behavior. They were especially concerned about persons who used the park as a campground although there were no sanitation facilities or running water. Some neighborhood residents complained about parties and late night festivities that kept them awake. A leaflet distributed to local residents by the park developers declared:

> We apologize, all of us, for any noise and inconvenience caused you by the gathering of people in the park the last two nights. The out-of-towners will leave soon, and those of us who live here and use the park will continue to work for peace and quiet.

A study of People's Park concluded that efforts at self-policing by the park leaders were ineffectual.[10] They could not control many of the park users who were transients and had no stake in the park. The result was that the police were called; this was followed by several weeks of disturbances at the park and elsewhere in the city. Some have interpreted the park experience to mean that user self-maintenance is only a utopian vision. I believe that People's Park was not so much an exercise in user-maintained facilities as it was in user-generated design. Although there were informal "leaders" among the park developers, including some prominent University of California environmentalists, they had no legitimate authority to develop regulations and policies for maintaining the park. There was no way for them to prohibit people from camping in the park or from playing bongos late into the night. A political mechanism for maintaining the park was missing.

The idea of user-maintained systems has profound implications for the design professions. One can imagine apartments, homes, parks, and neighborhoods designed to be maintained by the users themselves.[11] In my opinion, no automobile is manufactured to be user-maintained. The warranties become void unless the user brings the car into a registered shop for periodic service. Most technical manuals for the car seem to be written for servicemen rather than owners. It is very difficult for an owner to get access to the hoists and complex diagnostic equipment of an automobile

[10]A. H. Miller, "The People's Park: Its Social and Political Implications of Self-Generated Recreational Facilities," *Proceedings of the 1969 Park and Recreation Administrators Institute.* Davis, California: University Extension, University of California, Davis, 1970.

[11]Several local apartment builders catering to university students include in their advertisements the statement "no resident manager on the premises." My own (non-student) apartment building is run on a similar basis. The tenants are willing to trade off the minor inconvenience of phoning the owner when there is a maintenance problem, for the freedom and privacy resulting from an absence of custodial employees. Without user-participation in environmental decision-making, custodians tend to become managers.

repair shop. I know of no cooperative garages available where people can come in and use the equipment for a fee.

Only rarely are public parks and recreation facilities designed to be user-maintained. Major renovations, seasonal adjustments, and even routine maintenance are left to outside agencies. Nothing is left to the public except use of the facility under prescribed conditions. This forfeits the savings that can result from user-maintenance; it also widens the gulf between users and the facility. The residents of ghetto neighborhoods often feel that the parks don't belong to them. The result is a lack of community effort to restrict vandalism since the park represents the occupation army from city hall. User-maintenance is the only immediate remedy for littering and vandalism. Unless the people themselves want to keep a park clean no amount of maintenance or police surveillance can accomplish this goal.

Peter and Iona Opie,[12] the remarkable English couple who have spent a lifetime collecting children's games and stories from around the world, have negative opinions about most children's playgrounds. They think they are designed to fit adult misconceptions about the nature of children's play. The adult seems to presume that children have few diversions of their own, are incapable of self-organization, have become addicted to spectator amusements, and will languish if left to rely on their own resources. Thus he plans a closely-supervised, fenced, asphalt-covered yard where children can be watched and controlled. The Opies have found that children's games in cooped-up playgrounds tend to be more aggressive than those in more open spaces. The children prefer to play in the streets, the fields and the "secret places." To a child the best parts of a park are those that are least maintained by adults. An alternative is the adventure playground which is designed to be adult-supervised but child-maintained.

Because it is located close to where I live, I have been interested in the Putah Creek Fishing Access as an example of an adult-maintained facility. It also demonstrates the minipark concept advocated by William Whyte[13] for odd-sized city spaces, railroad right-of-ways, city easements, old stream beds, arroyos, and the rooftops of public buildings. Many small spaces exist even in heavily populated areas. Their recreational or park potential has been overlooked in the search for larger and more impressive spaces. The secret of a successful minipark is neighborhood or user participation in development and maintenance. A minipark does not justify round-the-clock maintenance so the users must be involved if the park is to succeed.

The Putah Creek Fishing Access is a strip of land, about 2 miles long

[12]Robert Cowley, "Their Work Is Child's Play," *Horizon*, Winter, 1971, **XIII**, pp. 14–15. See also Peter and Iona Opie, *Children's Games in Street and Playground*. Oxford: Clarendon Press, 1969.

[13]William H. Whyte, *The Last Landscape*. Garden City: Doubleday & Company, Inc., 1968.

The architect's role in designing buildings is often secondary to the role played by client syndicates, banks, and contractors. On this project the architect didn't even rate a plaque—or perhaps he didn't want one.

with a maximum width of 500 feet, lying between Putah Creek and California Highway 128. It is divided into three contiguous miniparks, each with a separate entrance. The banks of the creek are crowded with vegetation, with small cleared areas occurring now and then, laced with small paths made by fishermen and picnickers. Before 1963 the area was owned by the Glide Ranch. Its owners had opened the area to the public, and it was used regularly for fishing, picnicking, and some camping. In 1963 a man was shot and killed in the park area; the mystery of this murder has never been solved. Because of this incident, and the problem of litter, the Glide Ranch owners closed the land to the public. Fishermen consequently put a great deal of pressure on the county to reopen the area. The county consulted with the California Wildlife Conservation Board which bought the land from the Glide Ranch and added the access roads, parking lots, chemical toilets, and tables. The county signed a contract with the board agreeing to maintain the park. Park maintenance is now under contract to a private citizen who is responsible for opening and closing the park and emptying the baskets, but he is not physically present during the day. In regard to litter, vandalism, and safety, the emphasis is on self-maintenance by the users. In 1969 Stephen Corey, a student of mine, conducted a survey of users of this park and found them pleased with the area as it was. Many voiced their reluctance to see it developed further, since this might change its character as a picnic and fishing area. Most people had no complaints about the area at all, but some mentioned the presence of insects and the litter. It is noteworthy that persons spoke of "the thoughtlessness of people who littered" rather than of poor maintenance. They recognized that it was the task of the users to maintain the area.

User-generated facilities such as people's parks have been criticized for their seeming disrespect for private property. Critics have feared they may result in environmental anarchy. User-maintained facilities defy union regulations as well as city ordinances. The underlying beliefs seem to be that people are incapable of doing anything for themselves, and that it is necessary for a city agency to meet every need in a public park. If property is private, the city is expected to refrain from interfering, unless there is some threat to public health or order, but if property is public it is the city's responsibility to look after it. This is a shortsighted view in an era when the distinctions between public and private are breaking down in almost every aspect of life. Although lip service is still paid to the idea of private property, a man must get a city or county permit before building on his land, improving his buildings, changing land use from agricultural to residential, or even burning away the stubble on his property. He must accept city easements for utilities and must accept the law of eminent domain.

Most of the arguments against the idea that every new task facing society requires a new government agency have emphasized inefficiency and cost. Other arguments are the degradation and the stifling of creativity of persons prevented from doing things for themselves. Another implication of the slogan "power to the people" is power to *be* people. Despite the determined efforts of Madison Avenue, people are not satisfied simply to remain consumers. The creative expressions of free choice and individuality while shopping at the local supermarket are not sufficient. The cherry on top of the consumer's sundae is being able to create, to mold, to change his surroundings, to leave his personal imprint on the world, and to affect other people and be affected by them. The supermarket is not the place for this. Items designed for user-maintenance cannot help but include provision for the creative expression of individual and group identities. When they have the opportunity to come together and maintain their park, neighborhood residents are likely to decide that certain play equipment should be moved from one place to another, or that sunshades will encourage older people to play checkers.

Victor Papanek is a good example of an advocate industrial designer. A recent article concludes that he is less renowned for *what* he has designed, although this includes surgical instruments and play environments for the United Cerebral Palsy Association, than *why* he has designed what he has. Whereas the prototype industrial designer Raymond Loewy has sought to make money for clients, Papanek has tried to show natives in newly-industrialized countries how to make money for themselves.[14] He goes where his clients are—at one time or another he has lived with Hopi Indians and with Alaskan Eskimos. Following the model of the advocate professional, he finds his greatest satisfaction from teaching others how to create.

Like the advocate planner whose primary client is the community and the advocate architect whose clients are a building's users, the advocate artist is a valid conception. He would be a professional artist who owes his primary allegiance to the community. Instead of painting his own murals on the sides of a building, he would try to catalyze teen-agers or members of community organizations into painting them. He would help them to secure paints and brushes, to make the scaffolding, and to select a design. A large-scale mural requires considerable coordination, and there is expertise involved in selecting weatherproof paints and finishes. Such a mural would be painted by and for the community. Its success would be marked by the satisfaction experienced by the residents rather than by an award given by the artist's colleagues. I doubt if there are many advocate artists in the United States. Some characteristics of his role can be found among

[14]Ann Ferebee, "The New Men," *Design and Environment*, Spring, 1970, p. 35.

People's Park Annex in Berkeley has an interesting variegated quality not found in more formal and manicured city parks.

some art teachers in the primary grades. Even then it is a rare teacher who helps children create what they want without worrying about parental standards of "good art."

Adopting an advocate stance does not mean remaining free of values or ethically neutral. It is naive to imagine a designer as a technical expert who drafts the pros and cons of various alternatives and does not make his own recommendations. This misconception is based on the idea that the designer will lose his credibility if he talks about complex social issues. On the other hand, when everyone else is making suggestions, it seems illogical that the person with design training and skills should remain silent. But, as an advocate designer, he has a single input into the design process.

The final outcome will be based on many factors that go beyond design considerations. It will be the advocate designer's ignorance of these larger social issues—such as the effect of a housing project on traffic patterns in the city, on the social fabric of the area, on employment rates, or on economics of the project—that will diminish his credibility in the political arena.

DeCarlo clearly describes the desire of the advocate architect to work himself out of a job.[15] He thinks future design decisions will be made entirely by the consumers in a process of continual polyphonic confrontation. When this occurs, DeCarlo predicts that the presently ambiguous and authoritarian role of the architect will be deprived of all its authority. The professional will still assist users with his special knowledge of materials, assembly techniques, and the implications of design decisions, but the decision-making authority will rest with the users. DeCarlo concedes that this is a long-range objective; centuries of alienation from design decisions have left the users with a numbed sense of design consciousness. The architect's role does not end with the design of a structure nor with its completion but continues to be involved with the persons who use the building and with their daily activities. When these people lack competence in facing environmental issues, the architect must help them gain it.

[15]Giancarlo DeCarlo, "Why/How to Build School Buildings," *Harvard Educational Review*, 1969, XXXIX (4), pp. 12–41.

CHAPTER TWO

Social Scientists Too

When asked to join the design team to produce design covenants, the social scientist normally cautions against his active role in design, preferring to set down user requirements and then participate in the evaluation of completed designs at a later date.—SAM A. SLOAN

Without meaning to, I have devoted the last ten years to working with design and designers.[1] When I began, the liaison between the social sciences and the design fields was in an inchoate stage, vulnerable to diversion, charlatanry, and faddism. Experts existed whose knowledge of human spatial behavior seemed limited to the territorial imperative, and some designers resented white-coated psychologists telling them how to design spaces according to basic biological needs. Architecture was to become the newest social science. Fortunately these tendencies toward premature scientism and a new dogmatism stayed within bounds. The need for greater professionalism and the need for sharing information in the design fields remained. Reflecting the Kleenex throwaway ethic and the desire for novelty for its own sake, design was in danger of losing its social purpose.

Visits to more than 30 schools of design, architecture, and planning, have convinced me that this generation of students has a new sense of the social implications in their work. Many of their professors and existing practitioners are unreachable. Perhaps some of them will come around eventually, but it will be the new generation that will rebuild the world. In architecture and other design fields, reorientation will probably begin

[1]*Design* will be used as a generic term to encompass architecture, landscape, interior design, planning, and other professions concerned with the planning and design of the man-made environment.

16

in the schools. As curriculum changes, so will professional practice. This is the real meaning of student power and indirectly the meaning of faculty power. In virtually every school of architecture, the curriculum has either been changed within the last few years or is under serious scrutiny. Some saber-toothed curricula are still designed to combat out-of-date problems, but these are waning, and the schools affected can take heart from developments elsewhere. The intellectual ferment in the design fields is inescapable.

The question is no longer whether physical design should suit the people for whom it is intended, but how to accomplish this purpose within the current organization of the building industry, the economic system, and regulatory agencies. Discussion has moved forward from what is desirable to how the profession can realize such values as user-participation and long-range environmental planning. In design schools across the country, the visitor sees the same geodesic domes covered with clear plastic, the inflatable structures, and the ponderous junk sculptures in the outside courtyard. The design culture has moved away from the glossy magazines, jury awards, irrelevant architectural criticism, Guggenheim fellowships, and the promise of jobs in prestigious offices toward furnishings for low-income housing, campaigns to save open space, development of child care centers, and housing for the elderly.

Among the older faculty members and practitioners, one hears the frequent laments that students "don't know how to draw" and "aren't learning architecture." There is some legitimacy in these complaints. I met many architectural students who were more interested in programming (i.e., describing the needs to be met) than in shaping the forms themselves. These new interests are a healthy development. Society would be the loser if every architect laid down his pencil, but there is no danger of this happening. Instead we are seeing the emergence of new roles and social forms to meet the changing interests and talents of a growing segment of architectural graduates. Firms now exist whose practice is confined to prearchitectural programming, interests in design research, awakening concern about building evaluation, uses of computers both in design and information storage, and attempts to develop a language for expressing spatial experience. These approaches are not for every designer but any one of them is likely to affect the architectural profession more profoundly than the approach of a designer whose work relies on the appeal of fashion.

There are always those who view new movements or new intellectual trends as a diminution of existing programs and resources. The ecology movement is seen as a diversion of energy from the black revolution or the antiwar movement, drugs as an escape from social problems, and rock music as a flight from meaning. By the same logic the concern with the social implications of design *must* siphon away energies that previously were used for visual representation, spatial awareness, and good design.

I consider this a false dichotomy. I believe the new ferment will enrich and guide design practice rather than turn designers into second-rate social workers and advocacy planners. The major tasks in institutionalizing concern with social factors into design education and practice are: (1) to develop procedures and programs in which user inputs can be generated from existing and simulated structures; and, (2) to develop means by which environmental awareness within the general population can be heightened.

We are beyond the point, if it ever existed, when a building could educate and inform by itself. A building has many messages for its occupants, but there is a difference between this sort of nonverbal teaching and formal education. The typical courthouse may intimidate a defendant from a poverty area and tell him that he is being judged by his betters rather than his peers. He may sense this intuitively, but the task falls to others to make these messages explicit and to answer the question of whether this is the kind of message a courthouse should convey. The reader may be disheartened by the idea that I am adding a new burden to the designer—not only should he be a social worker—he should also be a teacher. I hope the chapter on environmental awareness will show ways of overcoming spatial numbness, the self-defeating adaptation to an environment which is becoming constantly more ugly and polluted.

Listening to questions and comments from students, I discovered that my original message to the design professions was no longer needed. There is no point in castigating the lordly master architect, who thinks he knows what is best for people regardless of what they say, who never visits his buildings after they are opened, who is interested chiefly in the reactions of his colleagues, and who sees his buildings as great hollow sculptures that will remain fixed and unchanged through the years. He has his admirers as well as his critics. He may have been a giant in his time, but so was the dinosaur. While some designers look longingly upon his life-style, most students are firm in the conviction that buildings are for the people who use them. In a sense, all people in the world are affected by every building. It is necessary to determine the extent of that influence and to develop the political means for introducing user inputs into the design process in such a way that the influence of each group upon a structure is proportionate to its effect upon their lives. The difficulty of realizing this ideal does not make it less useful as a goal nor as a comparison point for existing decision-making processes.

When I wrote *Personal Space*,[2] I found myself performing a difficult juggling act, trying to awaken interest and develop programs in four major areas:

[2]Robert Sommer, *Personal Space.* Englewood Cliffs, New Jersey: Prentice-Hall, Inc., 1969.

1. Impressing upon architects and designers the behavioral implications of their work.

2. Making social scientists aware of environmental influences on behavior.

3. Generating user inputs in dormitories, hospitals, and airports, and observing how they could be applied in programming and design. The scarcity of useable information made it incumbent upon me to collect it. Fortunately I can now relax and begin to use other people's work.[3]

4. Attempting to reach space managers, those individuals who oversee the management and renovation of the built environment. These persons are less interested in methods for designing new spaces than in making optimal use of those they already have.

Looking back I realize that I had neglected a very significant group—the users of the environment. All the persons I was working with were doing things *to* people—designing spaces, arranging them, or studying user behavior. This seemed a trickle-down approach in regard to the actual consumers, who were viewed as raw material or as clinical specimens rather than as active shapers of a changing environment.

In my previous work the issue of user involvement arose only indirectly. Architects asked how people could be educated to appreciate good design and how residents of slum areas could be kept from vandalizing neighborhood parks. People became the flaws in the system—architects knew how to design good houses, hospitals, and parks, but people simply weren't willing to pay for them or to use them properly. The problem for professionals seemed to be how to get people to behave properly.

This problem may still be valid but the we/they dichotomy is not. We are all part of the environment—city planners, housewives, teachers, and salesmen—and we must understand the effects of our actions on other people and on our surroundings. A task at least as important as reaching designers and space managers is to educate people in the creative and wise use of the environment. Although legal codes and regulations are necessary, they can succeed only if they are accepted by the users themselves. This means that individuals must become aware of the effects of their actions on other people and upon the environment.

When I first began working with design teams, I believed that the main contribution of a social scientist to the design fields lay in programming, which meant uncovering human needs insofar as physical forms were concerned. My views were similar to those of Harold Horowitz in his article "The Program's the Thing."

[3]The most complete source book of work to date is *Environmental Psychology* (H. Proshansky, W. H. Ittleson, and Leanne G. Rivlin, eds.). New York: Holt, Rinehart and Winston, Inc., 1970. However, in order to locate the research on a specific topic, the interested reader must still return to the original literature.

The behavioral sciences hold great significance for the architecture of the future. They promise improvements in our ability to describe architecture, our understanding of the kinds of responses that occur in architecturally controlled environments, in our ability to predict the consequences of design changes and to evolve direct solutions for specific program requirements.[4]

This was a logical role for an expert in human motivation. However, as I encountered questions of stated needs versus "real needs" and realized the impossibility of knowing how a building was going to be used beforehand, I began to feel that programming seemed a rather idealistic and almost ethereal effort. One was often in the position of custom designing for people who were not physically present or who might not even exist in a meaningful sociological sense.

On the other hand, someone has to plan a public housing project even when there are no tenants or design a hospital without knowing the identity of the staff or the patients. Instead of searching for some hypothetical ideal —the average hospital patient or the stereotype of a welfare recipient—it seemed more reasonable to consider existing projects as systems in flux.

A fluid conception of time in the form-making fields is vital. When examining existing housing projects, one should look for what they are becoming as well as what they are now and what they have been. What are the pressures for change and what directions are they taking? At one time I applauded the creation of specialized programming firms. I thought that interviewing clients and potential users would result in a statement of the client's needs which the architect could turn into drawings and three-dimensional forms. Now I am pessimistic about the value of a service which transforms user needs into an absolute standard. I believe that the most relevant information will be discovered by evaluating existing projects rather than by asking people what they want. Certainly it is important to talk with potential users about a prospective park; it is also necessary to look at existing parks which are similar.

In the city planning field, particularly, a plethora of surveys, along with a dearth of ideas as to how they can be applied, is evident. Continuation of the present situation inevitably will bring the survey approach into disrepute. When consumers believe that surveys are substitutes for actions and that behavioral scientists are using them as guinea pigs, the amount of fruitful collaboration that can be expected is minimal. On the other hand, if designers and planners become overoptimistic about the possibilities of using behavioral data and if they commission extensive surveys without knowing how to use them, they are likely to be left frustrated and disillu-

[4]Harold Horowitz, "The Program's the Thing," *A.I.A. Journal*, May, 1967, pp. 94–100.

The 95-year-old lady shown here is complaining that she doesn't have enough light for reading. In dealing with people who are elderly, infirm, disabled, or handicapped, the environment should be prosthetic.

sioned.[5] As in any other endeavor, it is easy to become intrigued with the means and to forget about the ends. If this situation is not clarified, the legitimacy of behavioral science in the design fields and the credibility of the researchers will be in jeopardy.

One sign that a field is accepted, respectable, and legitimate, is the publication of a scientific or technical journal. The interface between social science and design now has two such journals—one, a collection of abstracts edited at Pennsylvania State University entitled *Man-Environment Systems* and the other, *Environment and Behavior*, edited at the City University of New York. A second indication of acceptance is the creation of degree-granting programs in the field. There are programs in geopsychology at Clark University, man-environment relations at Pennsylvania State University, environmental psychology at the City University of New York, design and environmental analysis at Cornell University, and various behavior-oriented programs in design schools. A third indication of acceptance is the formation of professional or scientific societies which are devoted to the problem. Initially these are small informal groups open to anyone with

[5]There is an important distinction between a *survey* of what people want and an *evaluation* of what they already have. Statements of preferences obtained in a survey are more meaningful as points of comparison and departure in the context of evaluations of existing forms.

an interest in the area; gradually the groups become more selective. They adopt more rigid admission criteria and increase dues. A quantitative measure of these trends can be seen in the Human Ecological Society, which originally charged no dues and sent out a free newsletter. A few years later there was a request for a voluntary one dollar contribution to cover the newsletter; this went up to two dollars when publication became more frequent. My dues notice for 1970 gave me the following options:

$5 Active member dues to cover subscription costs to the *Newsletter on Human Ecology*.

$10 Members will receive the *Newsletter on Human Ecology* and the *Bulletin on Human Ecology*.

$20 The *Newsletter on Human Ecology*, the *Bulletin on Human Ecology*, and the *Journal of Human Ecology* will be offered to members.

When I first began working as a member of design teams, I tried to keep each person's role distinct. I acted the part of the social scientist who could evaluate people's behavior in buildings and parks. Unfortunately this was not a very practical approach for programming new facilities. Not surprisingly, architects and owners are more interested in knowing how a proposed building will work before it is built, than in learning its flaws afterwards. There is a need for serious evaluation of completed buildings, but the present design process separates this need from programming. My long-range goal is to see this situation corrected—no design should exist without evaluation, and no evaluation without redesign. In this ideal arrangement the clients, consumers, and other interested parties will supply program inputs, and the psychologist will act as a catalyst and information specialist. The psychologist, who has no training in graphic representation, would probably make a fool of himself if he drew a floor plan. There is nothing objectionable about his discussing room arrangements, desk sizes, or preferred color schemes as long as he does not touch a pencil.

Life is never this simple, however, and good teamwork requires at least a partial blurring of roles in order to respond to task demands. It may not be sufficient for a psychologist to describe how tenants in a housing project want their playgrounds built—he may have to illustrate with photographs and drawings. The architect, too, must take an honest look at his role on the design team. Whether he likes it or not, he must become involved in client education. It is a myth that this can be accomplished by the building itself. People are not going to be educated by an office building that remains empty because of lack of clients or by a housing project that demeans them. A building is a meaningless abstraction when it is not considered along with people's expectations about it, its location in the community, and the prevailing social and economic system.

I believe it is quite legitimate for a designer to concentrate his efforts on a particular environmental scale. Obviously if everybody worked at the same scale—for example, city planning—we might end up with great cities but with tawdry neighborhoods, unimaginative houses, and bleak furnishings. There seems no danger of such exclusive preoccupations. The problem is rather that people who work at different scales do not come together as part of a single design team. Personally, I was trained as a social psychologist, and I am most comfortable at the scale of face-to-face groups or at least with people where there is some visual contact. Most of my work with designers has been connected with classrooms, cafeterias, public lounges, offices, dormitories, and rapid transit seating areas. On each project my own input was not sizeable, but I felt it contributed to the final design. When I helped an architect program a new airport, I directed my comments primarily toward the passenger waiting areas.[6] Other members of the design team and outside consultants supplied information about parking facilities, baggage handling, and the control of air and noise pollution.

I still feel somewhat defensive about restricting my efforts to a particular aspect of a problem, but the complexity of environmental issues is so great that I realize I can't do much more. The amount of information being produced is too extensive for a single individual to keep abreast of developments even in his own field. The only feasible solution involves design teams, representing a variety of disciplines and backgrounds, which can analyze all the relevant aspects of a project.

Fortunately the new designer tends to be interdisciplinary in outlook and approach. Without rejecting intuition and creative ideas, he directs them outward to the problems around them. The artist turns inward and translates his visions into paintings that are sufficient unto themselves; the designer must direct his creative talents to problems that must be solved, to people who are going to be affected by the solutions, and to other technical persons who know something about those problems. He is not a Renaissance man nor a designer for the twenty-first century. He is a competent professional living in the perilous but tremendously exciting twentieth century.

6Robert Sommer, "The Lonely Airport Crowd," *Air Travel*, April, 1969, pp. 16–18; also "Waiting Rooms vs. Professor," *Air Travel*, February, 1971, pp. 13–14.

CHAPTER THREE

Awareness

If this generation doesn't wake up, the next generation won't know any better. They'll think that swimming in filth is the normal thing to do. They'll think that the moon is supposed to be yellow. They'll think they are breathing clean air and drinking clean water because they won't know any better.
—DAVID BLAUSHILD

A common argument against introducing consumer values into the design process is that most people are unaware of available options and trade-offs. This point is well taken as far as it goes. There is no logic in asking people about geodesic domes or about inflatable structures unless they have had some experience with them. Rather than to exclude people from making design decisions because they are ignorant, the most feasible solution is to educate them. Many people have become so accustomed to ugliness and congestion that they don't know anything else. It is difficult for a New Yorker to believe that a subway system actually can be clean, attractive, modern, and efficient.

The standard dictionary meaning of awareness is to be conscious of something, to "take into account" an object or state of affairs, and to experience it. Awareness is not an either/or process since there can be various levels and degrees of it. In this chapter we will be concerned with awareness as the precursor of environmental action. People must be made aware of a situation *as a problem* before they will do anything about it. Effective action requires that a person adopt a problem-solving posture toward his environment. The traditional enemies of awareness are the turn-off processes —adaptation, habituation, conformity, and adjustment. These are also valid ways of handling incoming stimuli. There are times and places to adapt,

24

but we are in danger of accepting small increases in noxious stimuli to the point where the survival of the species and an acceptable quality of life are threatened.

It is important to include emotions in a concept of awareness, since we are talking about a live, dynamic, and engaged consciousness. Freud used a closed hydraulic model of motivation, with each person having a fixed amount of emotional energy. According to Freud, when this energy is not released through personally satisfying activities, it either becomes dammed up and produces tensions within the body (psychosomatic symptoms) or it warps the character structure through energy inhibition or uncontrolled energy outflow. Psychological defense mechanisms, such as rationalization and sublimation, are means by which a person handles energies which have not been discharged in a socially approved or personally satisfying manner. In treating neurotics, Freud was concerned mainly with removing blockages in the energy flow system.

More recent psychologists, especially those who identify themselves with the human potential movement, reject the model of a closed hydraulic system and accept an open and dynamic one. This implies a variable energy model which is less interested in directing the course of existing energies than in increasing overall energy flow. The human potential theories also stress an hierarchical arrangement of needs. Basic physiological needs such as hunger and thirst are at the bottom, and the needs for safety and security, affection, esteem, and self-actualization rise in ascending order. When the lower-level needs are unsatisfied—particularly hunger or shelter—individuals are not going to have much time or interest in the higher-order needs. Conversely, satisfaction of lower-order needs brings higher motives to the fore.[1]

The satisfaction of needs at any single level does not automatically reduce the general level of tension within the person; instead, it shifts his interests and motives up the hierarchy to higher-level needs. As his job situation improves, a man turns his attention to his home, to good schools for his children, and to recreational opportunities. Satisfying people's needs cannot be a one-shot process. This is why social upheaval tends to occur when conditions begin to improve. The authorities proclaim "See what we have done for you," but people look around and find other areas of deprivation. The long-range solution is not to keep people turned off, nor to establish a continuing committee to find out what can "we" do for "them," but to teach "them" to serve themselves. Perhaps we can learn how to serve ourselves at the same time.

The two models—fixed energy and variable energy—are central to any

[1]A. H. Maslow, "A Theory of Human Motivation," *Psychological Review*, 50, 1943, pp. 370–398.

discussion of environmental awareness. Whenever I talk with a group about the need to pay more attention to its surroundings, the question arises, Is it more practical for people to remain turned off in view of the magnitude of the problems and the all-encompassing ugliness? I can sympathize with this view. Adaptation, habituation, and turning off are valuable defense mechanisms. In the past, when people were unable to control their environment, it was necessary for them to tune out disturbing elements. Things have changed in two important respects. One is that pollution and ugliness are reaching such large proportions that the survival of the species is threatened. People are in danger of adapting to ever-increasing amounts of pollution, congestion, and ugliness in a way that follows the Weber-Fechner psychophysical function.[2] If there is no smog in an area, a tiny amount will be noticed; but, if there is heavy pollution, it will take a large increase to be seen as a difference. The other new factor is that adaptation to environmental pollution is no longer necessary from a technical or scientific standpoint. We have the resources and the technical knowledge to eradicate pollution and ugliness. Tuning in to the environment and experiencing one's surroundings need not result in frustration and despair. These are the only ways we can come to grips with essential questions of environmental quality.

The foregoing two energy models are relevant to the frequent charge that attention to the physical environment must necessarily be diverted from other issues. Some critics maintain that a secretary who decorates her office, waters her flowers, and hangs pictures on the wall, will spend less time typing letters, reading reports, and doing the rest of her work. On a larger scale, some writers see the current interest in ecology as a siphoning of energies from war and racism. Both attitudes are manifestations of the fixed-energy model, and in each case I find the logic less than compelling. My experience has been that secretaries who care about their offices and who create attractive workplaces are actually *more* interested in their company's welfare than secretaries who don't care about the state of the office. I have no doubt that there are some government officials who hope that the ecology crusade will divert attention from the Vietnam war. On the other hand, it is absolutely clear that the ecology movement is completely antithetical to defoliation and genocide. Young people seeking a clean world will not tolerate a dirty war nor a dirty ghetto. There is greater likelihood that college students aroused to clean up rivers and cities will take an active interest in broader social issues than that students who are apathetic to whatever happens around them will assume this interest. Whereas

[2]The amount of a stimulus necessary to be noticed as a change is proportionate to the existing base level of stimulation.

the fixed-energy model criticizes needless diversions of energy, such as youngsters being recruited into anti-tobacco campaigns for sinister reasons, the variable-energy model admires turned-on people, interested in what is going on around them. My grandmother used to remind me, "If you want something done, ask a busy man." On a college campus, if you want to mobilize students on a particular issue, your best bet is to approach those already involved in other issues. Eventually one must broaden the base and recruit among the apathetic masses; this should subsequently make the masses more receptive to recruitment to other issues. Within boundaries that few of us ever exceed, emotional energy is not limited quantitatively.

So much of a person's life takes place without any real feeling or involvement. The task of the environmental educator is not only to teach people *about* environment—to inventory its components, origins, materials, and interrelationships—but also to establish the connection between the person and his surroundings and to demonstrate how they affect his life. It is not enough to prove that noise, stale air, and high humidity have an adverse effect on work output. All too many laboratory studies, in fact, fail to show this, since the victims of such experiments redouble their efforts to overcome environmental handicaps. However, the question of whether a poor environment produces a decline in performance is not the main issue here; it will be discussed later in the chapter "Beyond Productivity." Our main concern now is the extent to which a person consciously attends to his surroundings. Pavlov[3] described this as the orienting reflex; he used the example of a dog coming into an unfamiliar room and sniffing, pawing, and exploring everywhere. Pavlov and his associates spent many years devising experiments to drive dogs crazy; they found that neurotic dogs would enter an unfamiliar space in a fearful and turned-off condition, go into a corner and sit down, or stand fearfully looking at the door. The neurosis had snapped the animal's orienting reflex.

There is a tremendous gap in our knowledge of how information is translated into action. The information explosion by no means guarantees that the information will be used constructively.

Information about the potential of nuclear weapons and the widening circle of their possession has not noticeably accelerated their control. Information about the toxic content of our foods has not changed the law, the behavior of manufacturers, or the habits of consumers. Information about pollution and the destruction of the physical environment seems to have produced a new level of sentiment, the pragmatic results of which remain to be seen. We need desperately to learn the conditions

[3]Pavlov, I. D. *Lectures on Conditioned Reflexes.* New York: International Publishers, Inc., 1928.

under which information leads to constructive and appropriate social action.[4]

One of the most disturbing aspects of a visit to Los Angeles is that, although the smog situation has worsened over the years, people talk about it less. Someone moving to Los Angeles might not be aware that there had been smog-free days even a decade ago, and a child born there now would not know what a smog-free environment was until he happened to leave the grey city. During a recent visit to Los Angeles I found a newspaper article headlined "Smog? It's been around a long, long time," which assured citizens that smog has been bothering man almost from the beginning of civilization and that so far he has survived (Star-Glendale *News Press*, July 23, 1970).

Three thousand miles away, the New Yorker has adapted to other sources of stress. A recent editorial commented, "People in a great city the size of New York live in such constant turmoil, frustration, and an aura of crisis in their day-to-day routines that when something as basically unsettling as a strike by most of the city's police comes along, the average metropolitan simply lengthens his stride a bit" (*Saturday Review*, February 27, 1971, p. 20).

When friends of mine first moved into a house about 10 miles from the Sacramento airport, they were bothered by the noise and billowing black smoke spewing from the jets during takeoff. But when I visit their house now, I am the only one who is disturbed by the noise and the black clouds. My friends have adapted to them; conversation continues as the jets roar by, and drinks are poured without a shudder. Voices are raised when jets fly directly overhead. I made specific inquiries on this point and found individuals are unaware that they do this. Two studies on the overall reactions to sonic booms reported that although people believed that the booms interfered with their daily routines and that they were a definite annoyance, few actually felt like complaining, and only a tiny percentage actually did complain. The majority of people who lodged complaints had actually suffered physical damage to their homes or shops.[5,6]

A survey among residents of Clarkston, Washington, who live near a pulp mill which subjected them to reduced visibility, tarnished house paint, unpleasant odors, and possible health-related conditions, found that 85 per cent believed that Clarkston was an "excellent" place to live. On the

[4]Robert L. Kahn, "Presidential Message," *S.P.S.S.I. Newsletter* (newsletter of the Society for the Psychological Study of Social Issues), November, 1970, p. 10.

[5]D. Carson, "Environmental Stress and the Urban Dweller," *Michigan Mental Health Research Bulletin*, IV, No. 2, 1968, pp. 5–12.

[6]James Swan, "Responses to Air Pollution," *Environment and Behavior*, 2, 1970, pp. 127–152.

other hand, when the residents were asked specifically whether air pollution was a problem in Clarkston, 78 per cent answered affirmatively.[7] A similar survey in St. Louis resulted in the same paradox that more people are "bothered" by air pollution than will acknowledge its existence in the neighborhood where they live.[8] This led Riesman and Glazer[9] to the conclusion that "for most people in modern society, there is no direct relationship between responsibility for having an opinion and responsibility for action." The problem is neither lack of information about air pollution nor lack of awareness about it as a problem, but the individual's remoteness from any action to remedy the situation.

The logic of habituation is subtle and insidious. If one can adapt to 10 per cent of some noxious condition, why not 12 per cent? If one can stand 12 per cent, why not 15 per cent or 17 per cent? In one building on my campus, I found classrooms which had 30 per cent more chairs than the rated capacity. The explanation was deceptively simple. If there were 20 chairs in the room and 21 students registered for a class, it was easier for the instructor to bring in another chair than to find another room. The following year, 23 students might register for a course in that same room, and another instructor would bring in two additional chairs. The net result was that chairs now lined the aisles and the podium area, and the rooms were stuffy and overcrowded. The difference between 20 and 21 students may not be noticeable. The difference between 20 and 30 is noticeable, but by this time everyone seems unable to return to the original situation. There are simply too many classes of 25–30 students scheduled for that room. Awareness includes the unhappy realization that there are some individuals who will inevitably have a stake in the conditions creating the problem and who will resist any attempt at a solution.

These examples are not remarkable, but I think they illustrate my point. In the Los Angeles situation, we can prove that smog is associated with higher levels of bronchitis and emphysema. A similar link was clearly established between cigarettes and cancer (and also respiratory disorders) without too much effect on people's habits. The smog situation is even more complex since each of the contributors to the problem—automobile manufacturers, local industries, and utilities—disclaims the major share of responsibility. It might be possible to prove that ear disorders and headaches

[7]N. Z. Medalia and A. L. Finkner, "Community Perception of Air Quality: An Opinion Study in Clarkston, Washington," *U.S. Public Health Service Publication 999–10*, Cincinnati, Ohio: U.S. Public Health Service, 1965.

[8]J. D. Williams and F. L. Bunyard, "Opinion Surveys and Air Quality, Statistical Relationships. Interstate Air Pollution Study Phase II, Project Report," Cincinnati, Ohio: U.S. Public Health Service, 1966.

[9]David Riesman and Nathan Glazer, "The Meaning of Opinion," *Public Opinion Quarterly*, 12, 1949, pp. 635–640.

are more common in households close to the airport. This might induce a few people to move to another part of the city or to wear earplugs when sitting outside.

The real solution, however, to smog and jet noise is not individual avoidance but political and legal regulations aimed at the source of the problem. The same is true of depressingly barren schoolyards and hospital corridors and of the tawdry franchise strips along city highways. Finding another route or ignoring the ugliness and congestion may solve the individual's immediate problem, but, if no action is taken to stem the pollution at its source, the situation will worsen to the point where people turn off completely and the survival of the species is threatened. I am not denying the value of studying the effects of noise, smog, or crowding. I am saying only that such research is probably not going to have much effect on people's behavior. People can adapt to the dire warnings of scientists just as readily, perhaps more so, as they can to the ill effects of cigarettes, crowding, and smog.

A recent newspaper article described South Dakota cattlemen and sheep ranchers, who spend a lot of time worrying about spring blizzards, mortgages, inflation, and getting their children educated:

> With so much to do, there is little time to concern oneself with such things as nuclear missiles dug into one's land as part of the giant U.S. defense system against attack. You must come to terms with and learn to live with the cheek-by-jowl existence to missiles, armed with warheads that could be sent aloft to demolish whole cities, or which might make your homes and children and barns and livestock prime targets in case of war. So to the ranchers, the missile sites have become just part of the scenery.
>
> "Subconsciously you are aware of the missiles being there, but you tend to forget them after a while," said Earl Waterland, who each day looks through his red chicken coop at the missile site on his land. "I was worried about it at first, but when a person first comes out here, he worries about the blizzards and rattlesnakes too. But you get used to them. There is no sense in a person worrying about those things."[10]

There seems some logic in distinguishing between spatial ignorance and environmental fatalism. The South Dakota rancher with missiles in his backyard knows about their destructive potential, but he is turned off. The citizen of Los Angeles knows that smog may kill him, yet he is turned off; his children may never know what a clear day looks like nor know that stinging eyes are not a necessary accompaniment of city life. The remedy

[10]Kay Bartlett, "Plains Ranchers Have Learned to Live Next to Death," *Sacramento Bee*, September 1, 1968, p. B8.

for ignorance is education—for adaptation, it is awareness that action is possible.

Another obstacle to meaningful change, in addition to ignorance and fatalism, is the Pollyanna attitude. No matter how bad things get, the Pollyanna believes that some mythical "They"—the government, scientists, or the large corporations—are going to solve the problem. It isn't so much hope as it is blind faith. It is always "they" or "them" who will take action, rather than "us," or "me" in particular.

The Jeremiah despairs of arousing enough people in time to do anything about environmental problems. He feels that this can only be accomplished by a disaster of great magnitude. He believes that nothing will be done until 1000 people are killed by smog in the Los Angeles basin or until 50 people are poisoned by the local water. Unfortunately there is little cause to believe that even a disaster will wake people up. The worse things get, the more difficult it will be to perceive a change for the worse, even a disaster.

The Tough Guy believes that the best way to make people aware of a problem is to rub their noses in it. Requiring the mayor and city council members to drink water from the local river may be a means of insuring water quality, or it may at least result in a rapid turnover among elected officials.

In Los Angeles County, however, people have adjusted remarkably well to the smog. A first-stage alert is sounded when the ozone concentration reaches five-tenths part per million, which is five times the State Health Department's recommended maximum. The citizens of Los Angeles do not take these smog alert days very seriously—freeways are jammed, factories keep operating, and stores remain crowded.[11] Local citizens are purchasing expensive home air-purification systems, smog-resistant paint for their homes, and new eye washes to minimize eye irritations. What would it mean to them to "rub their noses in the smog"—compel them to carry dead bodies down Sunset Boulevard? I suspect the people would merely draw their blinds and bulldoze more hills for cemeteries. Scare stories and doomsday predictions will actually increase environmental numbness unless people know what they can do to solve problems in a very immediate way. Some action is necessary to keep people tuned in.

It is not the purpose of this book to deal with problems at the macro-level of air and water pollution, urban blight, and congestion. I believe that one step toward solution, however, is to involve people in a problem-solving stance toward problems in their homes, schools, offices, and neighborhoods. These will inevitably mesh into larger environmental issues, but they are originally perceived at a scale where there is some likelihood of success.

[11]Roger Rapaport, "Los Angeles Has a Cough," *Esquire*, July, 1970, pp. 83–85.

Writing about adventure playgrounds, Clare Cooper states that "Something for the children" is a rallying cry with which few can disagree, and it is often an excellent starting point for community organizations which can later move on to more controversial issues.[12] The Mexican-American residents in the neighborhood around Garfield Square in San Francisco organized to improve recreational facilities for children and teen-agers; they went ahead, after they achieved their first goal, to planning model cities with improved housing, health, and other facilities. I do not perceive an unbridgeable chasm between efforts to improve one's immediate environment and solving problems at the level of the city, the region, or the world. From an ecological viewpoint all problems are interconnected. The important thing is to start somewhere. I would like to suggest that for most people the logical starting place is the person's immediate environment, where the scale of problems is manageable and the effects of his efforts are apparent.

In the United States today, a great need exists for inner quiet and stillness, for things perceived at a comprehensible scale, and for meaningful human relationships. The current hyperactive consumer-producer relationship is considered neither necessary nor desirable. Yet it would be illogical to argue that the solution to local problems will *add up* to a solution to national problems. This would be fallacious reasoning, since it would ignore valid differences between problems at various levels. But the awareness, the feelings of competence, and the social technology organized to meet local problems are indispensable to solving larger ones. If we do *not* solve local problems, we will probably never reach the point where we can solve international ones.

On the other hand, knowing how to deal with ugliness, urban blight, and crowding will not automatically end racism, halt the arms race, or encourage population control. Outside of the laboratory such direct cause and effect sequences hardly ever exist. This is another one of those paradoxes with which we must live. Everything influences everything else, but few things operate by themselves to produce a particular outcome. The sort of causality that was suitable for the nineteenth century physics laboratory is not appropriate in a complex ecosystem, where causality is indirect rather than direct and the shortest road to population control may be cleaning a local stream bed or mobilizing a community to recycle tin cans. The evidence from studies of environmental problems is quite clear on this issue. It is not lack of information that is at fault, nor an unawareness of problems in the abstract, but rather a sense of remoteness from individual and collective action. As the title of a booklet published by a branch of the Amer-

[12]Clare Cooper, "Adventure Playgrounds," *Proceedings of the 1969 Park and Recreation Administrators Institute* (Davis, California: University Extension, University of California, Davis, 1970), p. 18.

ican Association of University Women urges, *If You Want to Save Your Environment . . . START AT HOME!*[13]

Research studies from the psychological laboratory clearly demonstrate that the Weber-Fechner law applies to decreases in stimulation as well as increases. Any reduction in a noxious stimulus such as smog or noise will be perceived in the context of the existing base level of stimulation. It will take more work to produce a perceptible reduction of ambient noise in New York City than in Peoria, Illinois. This does not help us unless the Weber-Fechner law also applies to activities that deteriorate the quality of the environment. Evidence on this point is much less clear. If housewives are not allowed to buy nonreturnable bottles, will this be seen in relation to the range of allowable supermarket choices? Considered in the context of all the items that they can buy, the loss of any single item is a small reduction in freedom. The Weber-Fechner function would predict that consumers could readily adapt to a series of successive campaigns or legal regulations favoring ecologically-sound purchases.

However, the major problem is not the adaptable consumer, but instead consists of the industries, middlemen, and organizations who have a stake in activities and products that degrade environmental quality and impair health. Auto manufacturers have fought federal standards on smog emission; steel companies continue to pollute lakes and rivers with their waste products; container manufacturers continue to distribute aluminum cans; and motor clubs resist the diversion of tax monies into rapid transit for beleaguered cities. One cannot apply the Weber-Fechner law to industries and organizations as one can to individual consumers. A small change in an individual consumer's habits, if transformed into national regulations or policies, becomes a major change for the American Can Company or for General Motors. This may be true, but the attempt of the industry or organization to base its resistance to change upon the reluctance of the consumer to do without his particular product or to pay more for it is indeed questionable. The foregoing consumer choices *do* operate under the Weber-Fechner principle. A determined campaign by the Federal Government and the container industry could, without a major uprising, gradually eliminate nonreturnable bottles and aluminum cans. No one is going to take up arms because he can't have his soda pop in an aluminum can or because he has to pay an extra two cents for each bottle, thereby creating a popular small industry for children who need to supplement their allowances. In this manner the Weber-Fechner principle can be turned around to work for environmental quality.

[13]Available for 75 cents from the AAUW, Palo Alto branch, 774 Gailen Court, Palo Alto, California 94303.

CHAPTER FOUR

Environmental Workshops

Moreover, a taste, not to say a passion, for building must be engrained in the child. Mechanical toys and mechanized entertainment kill his imagination and initiative; the feat of putting building blocks on top of each other hardly taxes the brain of a monkey.—RUDOFSKY

The topic of environmental education is not new, although it has received recent notoriety. Most existing programs emphasize an appreciation of nature, the outdoors, or the history of the city and its buildings. The most recent trend has been to deal with this education at the level of the total ecosystem and to make children aware of problems connected with pollution, lack of green space, and the population explosion. The child cannot visualize a role for himself in the solution. The magnitude and complexity of the problems are likely to produce numbness and withdrawal.

Efforts have been made to bring the problem down to the level of the individual child or adult. They can understand that collecting old newspapers will save trees and that recycling bottles will reduce the amount of garbage that must be hauled away. There have also been numerous attempts to include environmental items in school curricula. Children are taken to the beach and forest where the interrelationships of nature are explained to them, and urban children study the city environment.

During the heyday of progressive education, an experiment was conducted at Teachers College, Columbia University, to teach sixth graders about architecture.[1] The children visited buildings in New York City, spoke with architects, made blueprints, learned to identify particular architectural

[1] Emily Ann Barnes and Bess M. Young, *Children and Architecture.* New York: Bureau of Publications, Teachers College, 1932.

features, read about the history of buildings, studied the geometry of different architectural forms, and designed a play in which they acted out and danced the spirit of Egyptian, Gothic, and other periods of architecture. A recent international conference on environmental education recommended the provision of gardens and landscape areas in schools, an adequate supply of plants and animals in the classroom, and the availability of nature reserves and study areas for use by students.[2]

Although it is important to develop a child's appreciation of the interrelationships in nature and of city settlements and how they work, it is also necessary to encourage him to use proximate spaces intelligently since this is likely to be his own responsibility. When adult rules require children to remain passive in regard to their surroundings—forbidding them to rearrange their classrooms or playgrounds—these same children are not likely to take an active problem-solving stance toward their homes or offices when they are adults. Rarely is a child encouraged to make changes in his bedroom; options are not revealed to him, and he accepts what is given as what should be. This is a case of a lost opportunity. The interior of their own home or apartment is one of the few areas of freedom left to the family. It can be used as a laboratory to develop a sense of freedom, experimentation, verification, and a keener aesthetic appreciation of one's surroundings.

In an experiment conducted at the University Nursery School in Milwaukee, Wisconsin, four-year-olds were given the task of planning their own classroom.[3] After taking the standard equipment into the hall, the group gradually returned items as they were needed and stored them against the wall. The center of the room became a "play laboratory" and the shelves were the supply depot. Conspicuously absent were tables which had formerly consumed space but had not contributed much else. The floor was preferred by the children for all activities, including eating snacks.

Rearranging a classroom inevitably runs into limitations of materials and money. The interested teacher can obtain some things by scrounging through her own possessions, by borrowing from friends, by checking the school storeroom, and by soliciting other schools as well as parents. The children at the pioneer Emdrup adventure playground in Denmark used what was available, brought their own materials, and when supplies ran short raised money to purchase items for the playground. Architect Sim van der Ryn is currently developing a service to provide inexpensive materials for teachers and students who want to redo their classrooms.[4]

[2]C. Bigler, "Environment Symposium Drew 20 Experts," *Sacramento Bee*, August 9, 1970, p. B5.

[3]Luther Pfluger and Jessie M. Zola, "A Room Planned by Children," *Young Children*, September, 1969.

[4]The Farallones Institute, 731 Virginia Street, Berkeley, California 94710.

Carpeted and properly sound-insulated, every bit of space in the open-plan school is usable.

Frequently the staff does not know how to use an open-plan school and teaches in a conventional manner. The result is individual partitioned rooms and a large common area which becomes an unused no-man's-land.

He is concentrating on surplus goods and throwaways—mill ends, pieces of foam, rug samples, and telephone cable. Using these materials as a wall covering, floor surface, or false ceiling can produce a more sensitive awareness of space, color, and texture. It is desirable for a teacher to create a classroom environment that is varied, attractive, and educational, but frequently this transmits a look-but-don't-touch message, and no effort has been made to increase the student's awareness of texture, form, or materials. When specific programs and exercises are lacking, the walls and spaces in a classroom remain background items.

Mayer Spivack[5] has developed a lesson plan for teaching children about the immediate environment. Beginning with the child's own bubble of personal space which he outlines with a circle on the floor, he shows how close together people can come before they begin to feel uncomfortable. Then he gives exercises dealing with depth, distance, and size. Children are asked about their memories of last year's room and how it compares with the present room, and they are asked to draw maps of classrooms they attended several years before. As a final lesson the children are asked to summarize what they have learned about seating arrangements and to decide on new ways for designing and arranging classrooms.

One of the most comprehensive programs for developing environmental awareness among schoolchildren is the group of lesson plans prepared under the auspices of the National Parks Service.[6] The programs are not restricted to parks or open spaces, but also deal with issues in urban and suburban settings. The basis of the teaching plan is the selection by the teacher and the students of an environmental awareness site which is studied by them in a fully interdisciplinary sense. The teacher is advised to:

> Plan a program which is well beyond the do's and don'ts of conservation behavior. Start with an examination of the student's surroundings—make the program relevant to the "known" environmental situations so that *appreciation* (cognitive, affective, and skills) begins at home. Examine the *use* of many kinds of places so that a comparison of large conceptual relationships can be made. That the constructive and destructive use of environment can be generalized and guided by judgments which are more than technological, economic, or political—that judgments include a sensitive appreciation of the environment and its future. The

---

[5]Obtainable from Mayer Spivack, Laboratory of Community Psychiatry, 58 Fenwood Road, Boston, Massachusetts 02115.

[6]The program is described in the booklet *The Environmental School*, written by Mario M. Menesini. The booklet as well as the Environmental Lesson Plans are available from Educational Consulting Service, 89 Orinda Way, Number 6, Orinda, California 94563.

awareness of a measurable environmental *value* system will develop from the weighing of effects that change agents bring to the surroundings.

The program emphasizes *cognitive appreciation* of the environment, in terms of information about local flora and fauna as well as human inhabitants of the area; *affective appreciation* including the emotional connotations of the site; *utilization* or the implications of the site for habitation, production, recreation, or waste disposal; and the development of an *environmental ethic* concerned with wise use of the setting.

As J. B. Priestley[7] points out, more science than ever is being taught now, but the subject is increasingly remote from everyday experience. Despite half a century of books, articles, and lectures devoted to Einstein's relativity theory, the general population has little understanding of it. Grand notions of ecology and interdependence and symbiosis are probably not generally understood either. If public consciousness about environmental problems is going to be heightened, it will probably be necessary to begin with more simple ideas like recycling glass containers and old newspapers or cleaning up a stream bed. The interdependency of environmental problems becomes readily apparent to anyone who has tried to work on them.

I would not overlook the possibility that simulation games or other innovative teaching procedures can be used to convey general notions of ecosystems to school children, since they do not have the same prejudices and sacred investments in the status quo as their parents. Children in a town like Arcata, California, can understand the connection between redwood trees, wildlife, clear streams, and man; their parents are unwilling or unable to look beyond lumber industry employment, welfare roles, and a familiar way of life.

Mark Terry is a young teacher and author of *Teaching for Survival*.[8] This small book manages to bring the principles of ecology—balance, finite matter and fixed energy, causality, overuse, and overgrowth—down to the level of the individual classroom. He describes how the teacher and his students can learn together to maintain resources and use them wisely. As Terry says, if ecology is not brought down to the level of the classroom, the final outcome is likely to be emotional detachment or hypocrisy. Many ecological lessons can be discovered in what goes on around us; in dealing with children, it is important to make sure that the lessons are ecologically sound.

When I was in high school, I spent the summers working in my father's handbag factory. One of my first jobs was to sit on a little stool next to the boxes full of scrap leather and pull out salvageable pieces. My father was

[7]J. B. Priestley, *Man and Time*. Garden City, New York: Doubleday & Company, Inc., 1964.

[8]Mark Terry, *Teaching for Survival*. New York: Ballantine Books, Inc., 1971.

constantly amazed at the amount of money that could be saved by going through the scraps a second time. I would retrieve pieces that could be used to make the smaller parts of flaps, gussets, tabs, and handles. My father was one of the largest manufacturers of reptile handbags. This industry provided employment for approximately 100 workers, most of them women, in an eastern Pennsylvania town. He made reptile bags because women were buying reptile shoes and wanted matching handbags. The skins came from South America, Africa, Asia, and other exotic places. As an adolescent, I never gave any thought to the survival of the particular species. There were always more alligators or cobras out there in the steaming jungle, waiting to be trapped by the carefree natives.

Now we all know better. Fortunately, American women no longer wish to carry alligator or lizard bags; this, in no small measure, is due to the dedicated efforts of wildlife societies and conservationists. Without the public awareness created by these groups and the subsequent laws and regulations regarding the use of wildlife skins, it is doubtful that many manufacturers could withstand pressure from store buyers to supply reptile shoes and bags. This is a small example of the way in which awareness is the precursor of environmental action.

Teaching environmental awareness differs from teaching ordinary subject matter. Information must be given on the connection between form and behavior; furthermore, feelings of competence must be developed in order that the listener can believe that his own actions will make a difference. Information is best imparted through lectures and printed materials; feelings of competence derive from involvement in action. According to Mark Terry, "Taking on the teaching of 'the environment,' so titled, is taking on a grave responsibility. Somehow the environment must be met, listened to, and worked with, rather than relegated to ditto sheets and textbooks."[8] A workshop or laboratory format concerned with local issues is most desirable.

Games and other simulation procedures can be used to teach environmental awareness. Gary Shirts,[9] who developed Star Power, a game of interplanetary decision-making, suggests that simulation techniques may have advantages over conventional lecture presentation. He lists them as hunches or hypotheses rather than as proven findings:[9]

1. Simulations can be motivators; they generate enthusiasm and commitment.

2. A simulation experience can lead students to more sophisticated and relevant inquiry, to question the resemblance of the "model" to the

[8]Terry, *op. cit.*, p. 129.

[9]Gary Shirts, *An Inventory of Hunches*. P. O. Box 1023, La Jolla, California 92037.

real world—and the greatest learning occurs when students construct their own simulations.

3. Simulations can give participants a more integrated view of some of the ways of man. They can see the interconnectedness of political, economic, social, cultural, and other factors. It can help them grasp the idea of a social or ecosystem.

4. Simulations can affect attitudes by helping participants develop empathy for real-life decision-makers.

5. Simulations affect the social setting in which learning takes place. The physical format of games, which demands a significant departure from the usual straight-row set-up of a classroom, can produce a more relaxed, natural exchange between teachers and students later on.

It is possible that these procedures, like any new techniques, can cause teachers to look at their normal teaching methods with a more critical eye. Lane and Sears[10] distinguish between concern with a problem and interest in it. "Concern implies some gain in a preferred outcome, it is future oriented, while an interest may apply only to measure of the present."

In order to create a problem-solving stance toward the environment, it is frequently necessary to remove stereotyped ways of experiencing things. A number of interesting programs use various sensory modification devices: *role playing*—asking the person to imagine himself as a man looking for a job and visiting the building's office for the first time; *simulation*—requiring a person to experience a public building in a wheelchair; and *blind walks*—asking a person to experience a setting blindfolded. All of these techniques have been used successfully to alert people to features of the environment which they might otherwise overlook.

School Workshops

Mark Terry provides an excellent list of experiments that can be done to sensitize students and teachers to the classroom and school building. Following an inventory in which the materials and components are itemized and catalogued, various experiments and exercises are undertaken. The easiest sorts of experiments involve deprivations of various kinds. Students and teachers agree to do without something for prescribed periods in order to learn how much advantage there *is* in a blackboard, textbook, or note-paper. A class can be conducted without plastics, glass, wood, or metals. Removing all signs and posters from the building would be one way of breaking down the tyranny of the written word. According to Terry, the

[10]R. O. Lane and D. O. Sears, *Public Opinion*. Englewood Cliffs, New Jersey: Prentice-Hall, Inc., 1964.

usual reaction to a verbally-controlled environment is to gather all the words into our heads and forget to notice the background. A building without posted words would be more likely to stand out in our perception. One of the most interesting exercises involves the simulation of a population explosion by adding chairs to the classroom according to a geometric ratio —one chair the first day; two, the second; four, the third day; and so on. A variant of this game, involving the entire school, has one classroom closed the first day; two, the second; four, the third; and so on, thus creating more intense population pressures in the remaining open spaces.

Here in California, Phyllis Hackett and I have been experimenting with workshops for sensitizing teachers to the classroom environment. Ideally, we would have liked to include students, parents, and custodians, all of whom have legitimate interests in the school environment, but so far this has not been possible. Following an initial warm up procedure, in which everyone introduces himself to the other people present, and in which we make an effort to break down the stereotype that we are going to lecture, we begin to focus upon the physical environment where the workshop is being held. For example, the participants are asked to notice how they are sitting, and then asked to rearrange themselves to facilitate group interaction. Typically this produces a general reorganization of the chairs away from straight rows into more circular patterns, and an ensuing discussion about the connection between seating arrangements and activities.

The next event is usually a session with an architect, either one who has been connected with a particular school or one associated with the State Department of Education. It is instructive to learn about a school from an architect's standpoint, since it quickly becomes apparent that school buildings are not always used as intended. Architects have their own educational philosophy, despite their protestations to the contrary, and this affects the physical appearance and workings of the school building. The architect finds that he can profit from feedback from a building's users, particularly when they are meeting together and interested in a constructive evaluation session.

The remainder of the workshop is devoted to awareness exercises and group discussions. In order to sharpen visual awareness, the exercises are done in silence. The participants are asked to really look at objects in the room, to touch them with their hands, to listen to the quality of sounds in the different parts of the room, to seek different vantage points and pay attention to nuances in perspective and lighting, to notice odors, and to adjust the lighting to see what difference it makes. Participants then reassemble to discuss their findings in groups of four or five persons. They return to the original classroom and adopt the roles of small children who are allowed to explore without any rules regarding order or cleanliness. They may rearrange or play with anything, and they should not be afraid

The school library on the morning before the workshop began.

of getting themselves dirty. The two workshop leaders act as models for the exercises, crawling on the floor, chalking words on the blackboard, stacking the chairs, building forts with the desks, banging on objects with rulers and pencils to see what kind of noises they make, and generally acting as child-like as they can.

The exercise was included in order to bring the notions of exploration, fun, and spontaneous action into the context of perceptual experience. The entire group then reconvened and shared its findings.

The teachers apparently understood very well what it is like to be a child, and knew that children need exploratory and open-ended experiences. They also knew that school systems, as well as customs, traditions, and the physical arrangements of school buildings, minimize those kinds of experience. Typical reactions included the teachers' feelings of helplessness in making environmental changes and their fears that interference with maintenance or janitorial procedures would not be countenanced by a budget-ridden institution which had set a high priority on cleanliness and efficiency. Several teachers expressed surprise at how different things looked from the eye level of a child, the change in room appearance from different locations, and the discomfort of attached desks and chairs. Some realized for the first time that they, as teachers, were free to move their chairs around, or to get up and walk around the room, whereas most of the children had to sit at one place for long periods.

Recently we have begun to focus these exercises on specific senses. Individuals are silent during the exploration phase; the participants meet afterwards in small groups to discuss specific perceptual elements such as texture, mood, variety, privacy, and excitement. For example, one group concerned with texture reported that every surface in the room was slick and slippery, conveyed the impression of being brand-new and never used, showed no human imprint, and had a temporary quality.

Such comments create an opportunity for the workshop leaders to introduce the idea of environmental messages. Physical objects have *emotional messages* such as warmth, pleasure, gaiety, solemnity, and fear; *action messages* such as Come close, Stay away, Touch me, Stand back, and Be careful; and *communication messages* about their own characteristics such as I am strong, I am stable, I am uninterested, and I am aloof. Each group was asked to record the messages they received from objects in the room. The ensuing discussion made it clear thát virtually everyone was dissatisfied with the arrangement of the library in which the workshop was held, and they were sufficiently turned on to want to change it. Since the principal of the school was a workshop participant, he gave his permission, even though he was somewhat concerned about what the librarian might say on the following Monday. Without any formal plan or organization, the participants worked as a team to discover a better way of arranging the room. The primary change was angling the carrels in relation to the wall, an arrangement that was asymmetrical to the floor area. The bin of phonograph records was integrated into the diagonal arrangement of the carrels. The circular tables were then distributed into a random pattern in front of and behind the carrels. Everyone agreed that the new arrangement was more inviting, less formal, made the room look larger, created more excitement because of the angles juxtaposed against the long narrow flow of the room, and developed more private spaces and choices for the children. An incidental gain was that the new arrangement of the carrels provided several centrally-located display spaces that had not been available in the former arrangement.

In another workshop the final exercise took place out-of-doors and was conducted by an architect[11] who invented an inflatable plastic doughnut he calls an *envirom*. This consists of a circular array of plastic cushions, each inflated by a single participant to form a flexible ring which can accommodate 16 persons comfortably. The participants lean back on the cushions and place their feet in the center of the device. This session was spent discussing the relationship of school architecture to the outside landscape, the functions of open space in the elementary school, the use of portable classrooms both indoors and out, and the place of natural elements in the school environments. There are advantages to holding discussions of indoor spaces inside an actual school building, where the subject matter

[11]Sim van der Ryn, Department of Architecture, University of California at Berkeley.

can be explored at first hand, and also advantages to discussing landscape topics outdoors.

A Hospital Setting

Holding an experiential workshop in a hospital, which is running 24 hours a day and dealing with matters of life and death, is very different from holding one in a school which is in use only from 9 A.M. to 3 P.M. on weekdays. It was not possible for us to have the hospital or even a portion of it for our exclusive use. The workshop had to fit into routine as well as emergency activities. We were fortunate to have participants from all hospital departments, including nurses, a doctor, the head dietitian, and a bookkeeper, as well as several board members. As turn-on devices we used such prosthetic aids as crutches, wheelchairs, and gurneys. These produced some interesting perceptual experiences which were shared with the group at large. Distances seemed three times as long on crutches as they had previously. It took a very long time to go down the hallway in a wheelchair; when one person wheeled another, the speed of passage was very important. Wheeling a person at ordinary walking speed seemed much too fast; the person in the chair felt as if he were a bowling ball going down the alley. Tall men were particularly bothered by being looked down on as they sat in the wheelchair; this did not seem to bother short men, who apparently were used to being looked down on. Riding on the gurney, a long flat table with wheels, made a number of people nauseous; the ceiling became the visual environment, and the overhead lights went flashing by *bang, bang, bang*, in a very annoying manner. A different perspective of the building was obtained when people took blindfolded walks accompanied by a sighted companion. This particular hospital differed greatly from the stereotype of emergency rooms in which people rush back and forth. The entire atmosphere was hushed and low-key, with slow movements, and deep background noises and rumbles. There was no hurry or rush; waiting seemed to be the dominant activity. Most voices heard were female. The hospital seemed essentially a matriarchy; the nurses and aides seemed to run the place, with men coming in and out as infrequent visitors. The physicians could be compared to a plumber or an electrician summoned to a home to fix something that was not in good working order.

Several years earlier we had taken students on blind walks in a mental hospital and had changed their stereotyped conception of the place as a wild madhouse. They thought of it, rather, as a quiet museum or rest home. Menesini used a similar exercise as part of a nature walk.[12] After the

[12]Mario M. Menesini, *The Environmental School*. Orinda, California: Educational Consulting Service, 1970.

schoolchildren have gone along a trail, they are instructed to stop and sit quietly, with their eyes both open and closed. Afterward they tell about the things they have heard, felt, and smelled. Eyes often see what a person wants them to see; they are active, searching out stimuli to support preconceptions; ears are more passive and in this sense provide a less biased source of stimulation. I do not want to overgeneralize, but there is no question that one hears more things in a different way when he is blindfolded.

An interesting sequence of topics is followed in most of the workshops. People begin by discussing what "they" (the others) need. About midway during the session the discussion turns to "us" and "our needs." The hospital staff members realize that the same items the patients require—pictures on the wall, nicely-decorated areas, and adequate space—also apply to them in their own working areas. Not only do they recognize that patients are people, but, furthermore, that we are all people and that what is good for the sick, elderly, or infirm applies to anyone. In a dormitory, the students may initially complain how "they" (the administration and/or the custodians) won't let them hang pictures on the wall, move furniture from one room to another, or paint public areas; after a certain point in the discussion is reached, however, they begin to talk about what they themselves can do to improve the situation.

Other Workshops

Landscape architect Lawrence Halprin and his wife, dancer Ann Halprin, have used experiential workshops to explore potential collaboration between their two professions. Events were staged in diverse locations, including downtown San Francisco, a dense forest in Northern California, the Fillmore Rock Palace, and the rugged Sonoma coast. The participants took blind walks down Market Street; they created kinetic sculptures using themselves, automobiles, and various city artifacts; and they built an entire driftwood city on the seacoast. The usual architectural problem is geared to develop spaces in which actions take place, but in the Halprin workshop the emphasis was on the action itself and on the ways in which body movement generates both architecture and dance.[13] Interviews with workshop participants revealed that the experiments "got the architects to move in space and the dancers to think about how to move space."[14]

Awareness exercises have also been used to sensitize Peace Corps vol-

[13]Jack Anderson, "Dancers and Architects Build Kinetic Environments," *Dance Magazine*, November, 1966.

[14]D. Bess, "A Strange Experience in Learning to Feel," *San Francisco Chronicle*, September 23, 1968, p. 4.

Workshop participants survey the new layout. The carrels were placed in a zigzag pattern to relieve straight lines in the room and to enclose smaller and more intimate study places.

unteers to the use of space in other cultures.[15] Teaching nonverbal communication is a difficult task since these cues are ordinarily taken for granted. Preceding one exercise, for example, the Peace Corps trainees are divided into two groups. One group is told that when they rejoin the other, they will be matched with partners, and that they are to establish a comfortable conversational distance with their partners. At a signal from the group leader, they are to come 1 inch closer to the partner until the conversational distance has been shortened by 6 inches or more. By this time, the uninformed partner will have experienced discomfort and probably will have moved back several inches. Both partners will have an emotional reaction—one to staging the invasion, and the other to the proximity —and they discuss their feelings about this afterwards. Emphasis is placed on the reciprocal nature of the discomfort and confusion. Argyle[16] found that Englishmen who were trained in nonverbal skills were more successful in communicating with Arabs than Englishmen who lacked this training.

[15]M. Schnapper, "Your Actions Speak Louder. . . ", *The Volunteer*, June, 1969, pp. 7–10.

[16]M. Argyle and R. Exline, NATO Symposium on Non-Verbal Communication, August 4–7, 1969, Oxford, England.

Many of the nonverbal aspects of the environment, both physical and social, can be brought into consciousness through training.

Artists have long used sensory turn-on devices to break stereotypes and perceptual sets. One familiar device is for the artist to look at a scene inverted by placing his head between his legs. Others try to imagine the scene in two-dimensional space, or to view the scene from an unusual angle, such as lying on the ground or from an airplane. Some of the awareness techniques amount to turning off one sense in order to enhance another. This is particularly true in the case of vision, which we rely upon for most of our information. Some estimates say that 90 per cent of all information comes in through the eyes; however, there are great differences between persons and cultures. Blindfolding a person ordinarily will enable him to hear sounds previously unnoticed and will permit him to be more sensitive to thermal and olfactory stimuli. The blindfolded person feels the temperature of the wall and the texture of surfaces around him.

Even after habituation or adaptation to odors or noises has taken place, the person may still be affected beyond the focus of awareness. Considerable research has been done on subliminal perception, or perception without awareness. It has been demonstrated that stimuli which cannot be identified by the person may still influence his behavior. George Klein[17] superimposed the words *happy* or *sad* on a face with a neutral expression, flashing the words at speeds much shorter than would permit recognition. Although the subjects reported nothing but a brief blur over the neutral face, the subliminal percept *happy* made the blank face seem happier, and the subliminal *sad* made it sadder. The words *angry* and *relaxed* influenced the faces in a similar fashion. It has also been demonstrated that the exposure of a taboo word at a speed too quick to be recognized produces a physiological jolt measurable by galvanic skin response.[18]

In his study of aesthetic ratings which took place in both attractive and unattractive rooms, Mintz interviewed each of the participants.[19] He found that only 29 per cent of the students mentioned the gross difference between the rooms. Another 46 per cent had some vague feeling that something wasn't right, but they didn't say that it had anything to do with the different rooms. For the remaining 25 per cent, everything was "fine," including the junk-filled janitor's closet. There was an interesting sequence effect in the results. Those people who went from the ugly to the beautiful room were

[17]George Klein, "Consciousness in Psychoanalytic Theory: Some Implications for Current Research in Perception," *Journal of the American Psychoanalytic Association*, VII, 1959, pp. 5–34.

[18]For a review of these studies see Chapter 13 in F. Allport, *Theories of Perception and the Concept of Structure*, New York: John Wiley & Sons, Inc., 1955.

[19]N. L. Mintz, "Effects of Aesthetic Surroundings: II," *Journal of Psychology*, XLI, 1948, pp. 459–466.

more aware of the contrast than those going in the opposite direction. A likely hypothesis is that the task orientation—the involvement in rating the pictures during the sessions—became so absorbing by the middle of the session that the subjects were able to tune out the room differences.

I would now like to tell you about the chair across the room from my secretary's airconditioner. Visitors generally sit in this chair. One day while waiting for her to finish a conversation, I had occasion to sit in this chair, and I was immediately oppressed by annoying vibrations from the airconditioner. They seemed to be aimed directly at the chair since they ceased when I stood up or when I moved to the side. I demonstrated this to my secretary who was quite surprised, since not a single person had ever complained about it. I have continued to bring people to her room, seat them in the target chair, and converse with them. Not a single one has spontaneously mentioned the annoying vibrations. Yet, once the vibrations are pointed out, the victim readily acknowledges their unpleasantness.

There is something terribly wrong with this environmental numbness. Apparently people are able to tune out the unpleasantness. But at what cost? I know that my ears ring for several minutes after I rise from the target chair. This would not be conducive to effective conversation or good public relations. Some years ago Abraham Luchins[20] assigned arithmetic problems, which could be solved by a long circuitous method which had been successful in previous problems. The last problems, however, could also be solved by an easy and obvious method. Most people had developed a set for the long cumbersome method and were not able to "see" the obvious solution. When he announced "Don't be blind" midway during the test, he reduced the use of the inefficient solution. A similar admonition seems desirable in my secretary's office—perhaps a sign "Don't be deaf." The ever-increasing noise levels mean that if people don't start listening, they are going to be deafened; and if they don't start noticing the smog and ugliness, they are going to be overcome by it. Environmentalists must reject a concept of "good adjustment" that refers to a momentary or cross-sectional condition. An immediate "good fit between the organism and its surroundings," accomplished by tuning out unpleasant stimuli, may eventually threaten the survival of the individual and the species.

Other methods of developing environmental awareness could be mentioned. Some of these, which would be too expensive or time-consuming to employ routinely, may occasionally be useful. Placing a person in an unfamiliar setting is one way to minimize preconceptions and stereotypes. The traveller returning to New York City from an extended sojourn abroad is struck immediately by its "brutal ugliness" as well as by the frantic pace

[20]Abraham Luchins, "Mechanization in Problem Solving," *Psychological Monographs*, 54, 1942, pp. 1–95.

of activity. These details seem remarkably sharp and clear for a few days.[21] This fresh perception begins to fade quickly, and in a few more days as the person adopts the life-style and tempo of the city, details which were initially arresting become less easy to specify. Spending a few days in a ghetto apartment or in an old folks' home can be an important learning experience. The goal is not so much to permit the person to observe how "they" live, as it is to provide more insight into the connection between man and his surroundings than can be applied in his own neighborhood. Although it may be easier to see such a connection when one begins discussing "them," an individual must eventually examine his own world if he is to develop feelings of competence in regard to it. Ideally, school problems are discussed in a school setting and neighborhood problems in the problem neighborhood in order to get people to experience the setting on an emotional as well as an intellectual level, and also in order to experiment on the spot with different ways of arranging and using space.

In this chapter we have attempted to develop environmental education at the level of the person in his immediate surroundings. This is important on tactical grounds for several reasons. The person is likely to be closely involved with his home, his neighborhood, his office, or his school. The connection between his own actions and a solution is more apparent. The likelihood of solving such problems within a reasonable time period is also fairly good.

Sometimes I accuse myself of ignoring difficult problems in favor of the easy accessible ones. In the short run, this criticism is justified. I know I tend to make issues immediate and concrete, to phrase them in such a way that personal action is possible and responsibility is clear. I have never felt comfortable speaking about problems in terms of some mysterious "they" or "them." I can *see* urban sprawl in the Sacramento Valley, faceless slurbs lining anonymous freeways, the beginnings of a smog problem, and too many speedboats at Lake Berryessa. Developing community awareness is not simply a matter of studying facts or figures but rather of stripping the blinders from one's eyes and finding an active mode of perceiving the environment. An action orientation requires that obstacles be listed in sequence as well as in a hierarchy of importance. First we must deal with the turn-off processes—apathy, indifferences, habituation, and perceived helplessness. Only then, with the community mobilized, can we remedy the conditions creating sprawl, pollution, and ugliness.

[21]P. Abelson, *Science*, 165, 1969, p. 853.

CHAPTER FIVE

People's Art

God bless the grass that grows through cement.—PETE SEEGER

Sometimes a design fits so tightly that it leaves no room for individual or group expression of identity. Even when there is consultation with users beforehand, a design may not allow for user inputs afterwards. This may be appropriate for a timeless monument which is supposed to express a given moment, but it is unsuitable for buildings which are supposed to fit people's needs and support their activities. Not only must a building respond to changing circumstances, social as well as technological; it must also permit people to express their individual and collective identities. When it fails to do so, we may see user inputs in the most elementary sense of direct environmental action. This issue will be discussed in the context of *people's art*, a generic term referring to the beautification or improvement of public spaces without the official sanction of the space owner or manager. This topic brings into focus important issues in environmental decision-making such as professionalism, neighborhood control, property rights, and the nature of art and architecture. Examples of people's art include vacant lots converted into playgrounds by neighborhood residents, fences around construction sites which have become graffiti galleries, people's gardens and people's trees, junk sculptures along the roadway, and driftwood sculptures along the shoreline. Its scale ranges from the couplet on a toilet wall to six-story murals on Boston's South Side.

The hallmarks of people's art are anonymity, fluidity, and neighborhood identification. Most often the identity of the artist is unknown and has become a matter of local folklore. Those who created them have left the driftwood sculptures of the Emeryville mudflats unlabeled and unsigned. They differed from those who paint rocks along public roads and seem interested mainly in letting the world know who they are, where they come from, and to which team or gang they belong. The anonymity of the driftwood sculptures indicates respect for the setting and the materials—the stillness and ugliness of the eastern shoreline of San Francisco Bay—raped by industry and freeways alike.

These productions have a fluid quality lacking in formally designed elements. The people's parks that have sprung up in various cities are constantly changing. When I visited People's Park in Minneapolis, built by residents of Dinkytown as a protest against a drive-in restaurant which would have changed the character of their neighborhood, it contained a large cross in memory of the students killed at Kent State University. The decentralized and heterogeneous layout of people's parks invites a user to add his own flower patch or bench or sculpture. When someone writes a poem and it is published in a magazine, the matter ends there. But when someone writes a poem on a construction fence, he expects others to add to it.

Direct user inputs usually incorporate existing features of the landscape and employ local materials. The People's Park Annex in Berkeley, located on the several lots owned by the Bay Area Rapid Transit and developed with their grudging permission, uses several car seats for benches, a discarded box spring as a trampoline, and old tires as swing seats. User-generated designs also tend to express neighborhood values denied expression through established channels and media. Architect C. M. Deasy[1] found that the most striking feature of the main walk at California State College at Los Angeles was the gaily-painted construction barricade around the new library site. Every inch was covered with fraternity promotions, political philosophies, student wit, avant-garde art, and personal pronouncements of timeless love. When he drew up development plans for the college, Deasy recommended that this opportunity for self-expression be preserved.

Formal art, generally a product of an artist's studio, tends to ignore features of the landscape. The large mural in the Sacramento State College cafeteria, for example, has an Aztec theme. The painting ignores the thermostat hanging on the wall—it simply remains suspended between two natives. A people's artist would probably have made the thermostat into a lady's breast or into a piece of fruit. The most creative graffiti embody and emphasize the existing features of the landscape. The cat faces along the

[1]C. M. Deasy, "When Architects Consult People," *Psychology Today*, March, 1970, pp. 55–57.

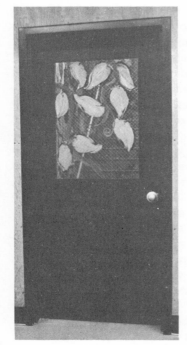

(a)

(b)

Outside entrance (a) to the fantastic stairway (b). Architecture building, Berkeley, California.

cement embankment of the Los Angeles River use the hinges of the storm drain outlet covers as the cats' ears. On several occasions the city fathers painted over the cat faces, but each time the cats came back, and now, apparently, shall remain forever. The sinuous mural in Berkeley's Wurster Hall began with a doorstop as the nose and eyes of a badger (formerly a profile of former French President DeGaulle) which was surrounded by a fantastic landscape, climbing three stories and culminating in a sunburst at the top of the stairs. Unless they are removed by official edict some of these direct environmental changes may endure for years. Others, like sand castles, are washed away in the tide. Chalk paintings on sidewalks disappear by the end of the day, snow sculptures melt at the first thaw, and dust drawings in abandoned store windows are erased by window washers.

Since it embodies features of the natural landscape, people's art is everchanging and ephemeral. There is always something new to see. On the sewer covers along the Los Angeles River, new cat faces appear as old cats fade away. The driftwood sculptures upon the Emeryville mudflats are never the same on two successive visits. The radical mural on the wall of the old Forum Restaurant in Berkeley, California, was recently halfpainted over. At People's Park Annex there is new growth to shrubs and trees, harvests in the people's gardens, new play equipment, a bulletin board for community projects, and a large bin for a clothing cooperative. Since there was no overall plan, changes are incremental and accidental. The park is a present reality with little sense of the future.

Although the nude pink lady painted over the tunnel entrance in Malibu, California, and the Berkeley People's Park became divisive local issues, innumerable incidents of neighborhood residents taking over undeveloped land for ballfields, footpaths, or gardens occur without visible repercussions. User-directed environmental changes raise the question of whether it is possible to distinguish between people's art and vandalism. The issue is raised by authorities who consider the changes steps toward anarchy and invitations to environmental degradation. Is it possible to distinguish between a person decorating a dead tree stump in a slum neighborhood and a person carving "C.K. loves Z.B." on a tree in a state park? Both acts represent the utilization of public space for private self-expression and communication with others, but the intent of the two persons is different. Hopefully the tree painter desired to brighten the cityscape and to counteract the drabness and ugliness of his surroundings. The tree carver did not express the anonymity of the true people's artist; his message, although accessible to any finder, was probably directed specifically to his girl friend. The artist's intention to beautify the landscape is what primarily differentiates people's art from vandalism and environmental desecration. A jury distinguishes between murder and manslaughter on the basis of the defendant's motives; the specialist distinguishes between work therapy and exploitation of mental patients on the basis of the therapeutic intent of the hospital staff in prescribing jobs for the benefit of the patient. Although subjective, the artist's intention is probably the best criterion for testing people's art. The boy who sprays a peace sign on the school wall or who chalks the name of his gang on a building is trying to communicate something to others and to express something within himself, but he is not specifically intent on beautifying or improving the environment.

Because these take-overs of public spaces are illegal, they are usually performed at odd hours by an underground group or by a single individual. The tenants of a housing project in Gladsaxe, Denmark, put together a playground in separate parts over a period of several days, before they assembled it at three o'clock in the morning. They guarded it on the following day in order that it would not be destroyed by the authorities; this had happened to another playground built on an adjacent slum site. The playground's popularity finally forced the Gladsaxe bureaucracy to accept it. At Cornell University the Plant Science Building was "attacked" by the Guerilla Graphics Group which painted brightly-colored designs in hallways and corridors. The secrecy involved in such activities necessarily means imperfect democratic decision-making. There is no possibility of polling all the occupants of a housing project or of a university about the sort of playground or murals they want because of the risk that the authorities would quash the venture before it begins. It is much easier to defend a playground or neighborhood park once it is completed than during its beginning stages. People's gardens and murals cannot be considered the pinnacle of democratic decision-making; rather, they demonstrate the failure of the decision-making processes in the larger society to take into account the interests of some user groups. For example, at the Gladmer public housing project in Regina, Canada, tenants are prohibited from owning pets, from creating a garden, and from putting up any form of play apparatus or enclosure for children, even on the portion of land adjacent to their own apartments which they are responsible to maintain.[2] Under such conditions, the appearance of a people's playground or a people's garden seems both inevitable and desirable.

The squatter phenomenon which came into being in 1946 in deserted British Isles army camps has the same origins. When useable buildings stand vacant one can expect direct actions by the homeless. The need for creative expression found in people's art is less obvious and pressing, but it will emerge sooner or later. Recognizing this, the authorities may attempt to co-opt and channel them. It is already possible to buy "Graffiti" brand fiber-tip marking pens in order to say, according to the manufacturer's

[2]Kyo Izumi, "Habitability of Environments," First National Symposium on Habitability, Los Angeles, May 11–14, 1970.

Authorities complain that the driftwood sculptures are a distraction to freeway drivers.

advertisement, "All the things you have always wanted to say"; graffiti wallpaper for the bathroom; and postcards and posters printed complete with cute graffiti comments. At Expo 70 in Osaka, Japan, a wall corner was set apart for scribblers and graffiti fans; anthologies of graffiti are published

Vandalism rather than people's art. Painted rocks lack the anonymity and creative use of local materials inherent in people's art.

periodically, and a syndicated newspaper column of one-line graffiti is used as a space filler by many newspapers. A firm in Mill Valley, California, sells attractive postcards and large posters showing the driftwood sculptures upon the nearby Emeryville mudflats.

Commercial operators look upon these direct user-generated forms as indications of a potential market for new products. These efforts at legitimization show a dynamic quality in American society to co-opt and incorporate new social forms and thereby channel them. Providing artists with a legitimate chance for self-expression within the larger system, yet benefiting commercial operators at the same time, increases the diversity of options within the society and also permits the self-expression, personalization, and urge for beauty which are involved in people's art. Public officials in several cities have taken the cue and have tried to obtain civic support for street decorations and public gardens. David Bromberg, a thirty-six-year-old urban planner in New York City, persuaded landlords to let artists paint murals on building facades at nine different locations. It cost about four thousand dollars to paint each wall; the money was secured from the Kaplan Foundation and from the New York City Department of Public Affairs. The Museum of Modern Art conducted an exhibit of color slides of those murals. The private developer of the Cedar-Riverside district of

Minneapolis gave permission to a young dental student to paint murals and supergraphics on various buildings and wall surfaces in order to brighten a drab and rather faceless commercial-residential district.

Street mural along Telegraph Avenue in Berkeley, California. Note the integration into the mural of the telephone lead-in as the vulture's head.

The authorities may also want to channel the direct expression of users in order to keep down maintenance problems. The librarian of the Widener Library at Harvard University placed pads of blank newsprint paper in the elevator; he hoped thus to protect the walls from graffiti. Unfortunately the artists would not accept the pads; they threw them down the elevator shaft. Giovanni's Pizza Parlor in Berkeley provides a blackboard and chalk in the men's room.[3] Construction firms have designated some of their barricades as legitimate graffiti galleries. A number of colleges regularly tack "graffiti boards" in dormitory corridors and Student Union buildings. Poet John Ciardi[4] was favorably impressed by the level of prose on some boards. He recorded the following sequence found on the walls of a California college. The numbers are used to identify a particular handwriting:

> 1) I have lost the equivalence of my ability
>   to live. Please help me find my way.
>
> 2) Be like Miss Muffet. Start with your curds
>   and your whey will follow.
>
> 3) Solipsist! Can't you tell a heavy question
>   by the weigh?
>
> 4) Encores away, my lads?
>   —USNA.
>
> 2) Yr lads are laid
>   Yr anchors weighed
>   And yr the fools yr mothers made.
>   —USMA.
>
> 3) All of you look like targets to me.
>   —USAF.
>
> 1) See what I mean? Send out an S.O.S. and
>   every S.O.B. within range jams the airwaves!

This sequence illustrates the dynamic and fluid character of user-generated designs—inviting, enticing, and demanding that the viewer involve himself. Perhaps it is this invitational character of people's art that makes it seem so threatening to public order. If not controlled or channeled, it would create a society of people changing the environment around them instead of tuning out. Even lamp posts, trash receptacles, and litter-laden

[3]One reason for the failure of graffiti pads is that their obviously temporary character inhibits serious commitment. What is the point of composing a poem for a men's room blackboard, if it is going to be erased in an hour? If one writes directly on the wall it may be several days or weeks before the janitor washes it off.

[4]John Ciardi, "Manner of Speaking," *Saturday Review*, May 16, 1970, p. 10.

streets would become alive with possibilities, full of potential for beauty and personal expression. The passerby might be moved to repaint the trash can, hang a mobile from the lamp post, and create junk sculpture with the litter.

User-generated design flourishes in times of social upheaval. During the tortured spring of 1970, the Architecture Building of the University of California, Berkeley, became virtually a graffiti gallery—posters, slogans, and sign-up sheets everywhere; the students at the University of Connecticut occupied the ROTC building and decorated it with green, blue, yellow, orange and pink psychedelic designs; and Yale University students, protesting the trial of Black Panthers, occupied the first three floors of the burned-out Arts and Architecture Building and decorated the central space with guerilla graphics. While the authorities may view these manifestations of direct user-involvement in environmental change as threats to the status quo, one can also see them as the emergence of new social and architectural forms. Guerilla theater, with its emphasis on participation and spontaneity, attempts to break down the distinction between actor and onlooker by bringing plays into the streets, where the neighborhood becomes the stage and the local people the actors.

People's art raises important issues concerning the amount of user-participation that is necessary for an acceptable quality of life. Living in an apartment, a child (or adult) will never have the opportunity to plant a tree, to see it grow taller than himself, and to stand under its branches and realize that he played a part in its growth. City dwellers not only need parks in which to walk, to picnic and to sit under trees; they need places where they can actually create parks and plant trees.

Man must be more than a consumer, even a tasteful consumer, of other people's products. According to psychiatrist Matt DuMont, "The extent to which a person can influence his environment will determine his ability to perceive himself as a separate human being." An account of the Berkeley People's Park stated that the park's importance to the young street people was not simply its status as a park or its location but the fact that it was an outgrowth of their own labor and decision-making. The park was something they had created and something in which they had a voice, not something that was created for them.[5] To be fully human means to create as well as to choose, to make things beautiful as well as to admire beauty. Some architects will go so far as to select a client's dishes, silverware, and ashtrays, and some interior designers will prescribe desk sizes, chair styles,

[5]A. H. Miller, "The People's Park: Its Social and Political Implications of Self-Generated Recreational Facilities," *Proceedings of the 1969 Park and Recreation Administrators Institute.* Davis, California: University Extension, University of California, Davis, 1970.

Creative use of local materials
in People's Park Annex.

and the model of desk calendars to be used in an office. A passive client
may try to live up to the designer's expectations and to shape himself to
fit the building; the probable result, however, will be individual and corporate subversion of the designer's plans after occupancy. A vice-president
may requisition a chair that suits his frame more than the decor, calendars
and charts will go up over the glass partitions to give the occupants a sense
of privacy, and pictures of children and wives will appear on the desks,
despite company regulations to the contrary.

The solution is not to eliminate planning but to plan for freedom. However creative and comprehensive, a master plan should give the opportunity
to individual consumers to exercise options in creating environments that
suit their unique needs. A man has to win a battle somewhere. If his office
location, desk size, and drapes are selected for him, he should at least be
able to choose his own chair. This may not seem important to the designer;
it is important to the occupant and is necessary for effective use of space.
Designs should not be so tight and confining that they preclude acts of
spontaneous individual creation. Not only individual needs but also rapid

technological changes indicate the value of a *loose fit* between form and function—the designer's concept of what a person's world should be and how it is designed. There must be elbowroom and footroom in designs to give people a place to be creative forces in their environment rather than components of a design scheme. Good planning allows for this freedom and, in fact, encourages it. Personalization does not detract from a good overall plan but rather enhances it. One sees not only a beautiful office layout or neighborhood plan but also creative and active people who feel an organic connection with an environment which permits them to create as well as to coexist and to adapt.

These user-generated designs can be seen as a reaction against unresponsive and unmoving institutions. The people who built People's Park in Berkeley had attempted to get official approval to convert the littered and vacant area into a park. When they were stymied by delays and denials, they took direct action. Many of the illegal murals and guerilla graphics on college campuses were created only after a long frustrating bout with officialdom. This sort of direct action in the face of unresponsive institutions has the tempting quality of moving quickly to the heart of the issue. Unfortunately, shortcut politics has its own problems—frequently making the threat to public order the number one issue—but it does have its appeal, particularly to young people. To paraphrase John Locke, when conditions are intolerable, you take things into your own hands, and, if God is on your side, then you win. To officials, the expression *power to the people* produces the image of a faceless and thoughtless mob following the leader with the catchiest slogan or the loudest bullhorn. The actual meaning of the slogan, however, depends upon the sort of power one is discussing and how it is to be exercised. The statement that people should have a share in making decisions that affect them does not have the same threatening connotations.

In order to find a solution to people's parks and graffiti, one must go beyond seeing the artwork itself as the problem. These direct user inputs are a visible manifestation of needs for creative activity, self-expression, the desire to personalize space, and the expression of certain aesthetic or social values. When there is a *problem*, it usually involves the reaction of other people to the artwork. They may be offended by what has been written or painted. In spite of scatological and infantile comments on some toilet walls, offense to the sensibilities of the observer does not seem a major issue. The nude human form has always been a favorite subject among artists, and people's artists are no exceptions. Although some persons believe that paintings or sculptures of nudes belong in museums, others argue that some of the best tavern art and garden sculptures involve the sympathetic portrayal of the nude female form. For the most part, it is not the content of the people's art that offends, but the feeling that public space has been wrongfully used for this purpose.

Trees in a Mexican-American
neighborhood in Los Angeles
are trimmed to resemble circus
animals. There is no reason
why all parks must fit a single
standard of regularity and symmetry.

Western culture has frequently viewed the expression of creative impulses as a threat to the established social order. The ideal society should involve an inevitable and necessary state of dynamic tension between free expression on the one hand, and social order on the other. If one person's actions infringe upon the rights of his neighbors, these actions must be questioned. When such discussion (and tension) is absent, it means that the social order is stagnant, or that people are so turned off to one another that they don't care what goes on around them. Berkeley authorities tolerated an empty litter-strewn field for several years; yet as soon as local residents planted trees and flowers and converted it into a park, police were called in. Clearly, the issue was the threat to the public order. I firmly believe that our democratic society can and must be constructed in such a way that it permits the expression of the impulses seen in people's art. Users of the environment must be more than consumers—they must be the creators and participants in decisions that affect them.

The questions concerning the extent of this participation, when it will occur, who will be involved, and how the decisions will be enforced, can be resolved only on a local level. Students in a dormitory could be given the authority to decorate their hallways, stairwells, lounges, and the cafeteria. The decor of the classrooms and academic buildings might be the responsibility of the Art Department and an appropriate committee of building users. A different procedure might be developed for a neighborhood in the central city. A group of local residents might be elected to establish control over all aspects of the visual environment. Sign ordinances, the color and style of light fixtures, hydrants, and billboards would be under their auspices. Why should all light fixtures be dark green or grey, particularly if the neighborhood residents prefer warm colors? A Japanese minipark and meditation center in San Francisco, with a rock garden and a Japanese-style bridge, was constructed by unemployed youths. I was delighted to find that the neighborhood park on Olvera Street, a historic Mexican-American neighborhood in Los Angeles, contained sculptured trees similar to those I had seen outside Mexico City. The workmen who maintained the center strip on the highway between Mexico City and Cuernavaca had shaped several of these trees to form birds. On Olvera Street the trees were shaped to resemble circus animals. Trees in neighborhood parks certainly need not be maintained according to downtown standards of neatness and symmetry.

Describing the vest-pocket parks built with the assistance of community residents, former New York City Park Commissioner Thomas Hoving[6] admitted that, by middle class standards, they were neither spotless nor

[6]T. P. S. Hoving, "Think Big About Small Parks," *New York Times Magazine,* April 10, 1966.

elegant. However, the neighborhood residents generally liked them, vandalism was negligible, and they were a vast improvement over the filth and rubble which had been there before. Whereas the present system encourages visual anarchy, community control might bring some order on the basis of neighborhood values. The sides of buildings would be public property just as the air space along freeways can be kept unobstructed by state or local laws. A neighborhood might decree that no advertising could be painted on the sides of buildings or it might encourage murals or mosaics expressing local values.

One can imagine a local council publicizing the proposal for a mural, advertising it in the local paper, and leaving a scale model or drawings of it on the site with ample space left for people's comments. If the mural turns out to be an acknowledged failure, the solution would be to get another group to paint a better mural. One can foresee neighborhood corporations or community councils with jurisdiction over environmental issues. There are playgrounds in Scandinavia where the children elect their own mayor and councilmen from among those using the playground. Special committees are charged with maintenance, sports, animal care, and parties. The original adventure playground at Emdrup, near Copenhagen, received a number of obsolete telephones, and the children installed them in their self-made playhouses. When funds and materials for the playground were in short supply, the children collected and sold old newspapers and scrap materials, and staged theater performances to raise money. It was their playground and they worked to keep it.[7] The goal of neighborhood involvement in such issues is a more humane and fitting environment. As the designer shifts his role to working with community groups rather than doing things for them, he will find that he learns almost as much from his clients as he is able to teach them.

I would like to add a final note of caution concerning the dangers in romanticizing people's art. It is neither better nor worse art than that created through legitimate channels. The People's Parks in Berkeley and Minneapolis had an interesting variegated quality that is lacking in most official parks, but I would not describe them as beautiful or stately. Some poems on toilet walls are highly creative, but most of them range from mediocre to terrible. While completing this chapter I heard an excellent talk by David Lowenthal on "The Environmental Crusade: Ideals and Realities," in which he expressed some harsh thoughts about people who expect instant solutions to complex problems. As Lowenthal put it, "Oversimplification leads to extinction both in nature and in human society." I

[7]H. B. Olsen, "Environments for Creative Play," *Proceedings of the 1969 Park and Recreation Administrators Institute.* Davis, California: University Extension, University of California, Davis, 1970.

must confess to some of the same misgivings about the heated rhetoric that surrounded People's Park; this should not obscure, however, the important issues in user-generated and user-maintained design. Most American cities could benefit from the experience of Amsterdam with its people's gardens along the railroad tracks and canal banks. These neat flower-rimmed plots are a far cry from the litter-strewn open sewers along the railroad tracks into New York City. If people were allowed to use the land it could be no worse and undoubtedly would be better than this.

CHAPTER SIX

Space-Time

The size of a park is directly related to the manner in which you use it. If you are in a canoe traveling at three miles an hour, the lake on which you are paddling is ten times as long and ten times as broad as it is to the man in the speed boat going thirty. . . . Every road that replaces a footpath, every outboard motor that replaces a canoe paddle, shrinks the area of the park.—PAUL BROOKS

Architects, city planners, and other form makers are acknowledged to be competent in making space allocations, but there is no single group of professionals responsible for designing time-worlds. Historians record the rise and fall of civilizations over time; yet time measured by the notches on the stick or the calendar markings on the wall remains a backdrop to experience. The horologist is a gadgeteer who has little interest in the thing being measured.[1] In Western thought, time is as important a resource as space. Americans are always short of time; a San Francisco radio station announces the exact time 932 times a week.

Discussions of time are limited by our lack of a suitable vocabulary. Our words are static and structured, whereas time requires movement and fluidity. Time is built into every sentence, and every object has time attributes.[2] It is so pervasive a dimension that it is difficult to objectify in spatial terms and difficult to consider apart from oneself. Time has been identified with space,[3] with movement through space,[4] and the unreality of both space

[1] W. Zelinsky, "Of Time and the Geographer," *Landscape*, Winter, 1965–66, pp. 21–22.

[2] W. V. Quine, *Word and Object*. New York: John Wiley & Sons, Inc., 1960.

[3] R. Taylor, "Spatial and Temporal Analogies and the Concept of Identity," *Problems of Space and Time*, ed. J. C. C. Smart. New York: The Macmillan Company, 1964.

[4] W. D. Ross, ed., *The Student's Oxford Aristotle* (New York: Oxford University Press, Inc., 1942), p. 219.

and time have been asserted.[5] In another sense, it is not time itself that is of concern to us, but the exchange between the person and his environment. Time is what we do over time—our sequential acts. Time is only a resource because it limits our transactions. Adaptation to a color is a response over time, not because of time.

Time can be fixed at a particular point by means of photography, sound recording, and the daily newspaper. A moment is captured; with imagination, it can be recreated at other places and at other times. One can also slow down the flow of time and extend the present by use of drugs, hypnosis, and auto-suggestion. The present is neither a point nor a plane but it is a pontoon bridge resting upon the river of time. The present cannot interrupt the forward flow of time but it can provide another plane of experience. Time is seen as a medium, a fluid, a great void. It is like lava, hardening as it cools, with the red-hot part continuing to stretch forward. Time is ubiquitous, insidious, and pervasive in human experience. It infiltrates the language and is the backdrop for all action. All buildings are seen and experienced in a time frame. It is tempting to continue in this vein, but it is *not* the purpose of this chapter to discuss the nature of time. Philosophers and physicists have territorial claims on this topic; I gladly leave it to them. I will devote myself to the relevance of time to environmental experience and action. The movement to maintain and improve environmental quality needs to operate on several different time scales simultaneously—from an immediate assault on pollution problems and unchecked population growth to a long-range reconstruction of society in a better relation with environment.[6]

In visual perception, a two-dimensional image is projected onto the retina; we infer the third dimension of depth. It is not often recognized that a fourth dimension—time—is also built into our percepts. I disagree with J. B. Priestley who, if I read him correctly, denies perceptual characteristics to temporal dimensions.[7] He doubts that past, present, or future can be regarded as qualities of objects or events. I believe that we perceive something with the knowledge that it is there *now*, and that this is different from our memories of something we have seen in the past or our ideas of what we may see in the future. The nowness of perception does not contradict the idea that I see something as "an old building" or as a design that is ahead of its time. If objects and events are perceived in a time frame, as I believe they are, it seems correct to speak of time as a perceptual quality—not simply duration, but temporal experience in the broadest sense as an ingre-

[5]F. H. Bradley, *Appearance and Reality*. Oxford: Clarendon Press, 1930.

[6]Kenneth J. Hare, cited in John S. Steinhart and Stacie Cherniack, *The Universities and Environmental Quality*, a report of the Office of Science and Technology, Executive Office of the President, September 1969, p. 6.

[7]J. B. Priestley, *Man and Time*. Garden City, New York: Doubleday & Company, Inc., 1964.

The newest and "best" of the veterans hospitals.

The lack of a language of spatial experience encourages such antihuman spaces.

dient of immediate perception. I looked for an English term that might make this time-dimension more explicit but was handicapped by the fact that in the English language *time* is expressed by verbs rather than by nouns. In German, compound verb-nouns are more acceptable. The term *Verlaufwahrnehmung* ("perception of the passage of time") comes close to describing how we see process as well as structure.

The politician acknowledges that there are still problems in the ghetto but declares, "Look how far you people have come in the last 20 years." The conservationist sees Lake Tahoe as it was when John Muir gazed upon it, as it is presently being developed by real estate promoters, and as it is likely to look in 50 years if development is not controlled. The hologram is a laser photograph which shows an object as seen from all 360 degrees. It would be useful to have time holograms that would show objects or events from their origin to their decay.

The Western notion that every act can be fixed in time with a beginning and an end helps explain the views that architecture is great hollow sculpture and that the city is a great stage on which the human drama is played. Without denying the aesthetic or educational values of good design, we must state clearly that architecture, city planning, industrial design, and all the other design professions differ from the fine arts in important respects. Unlike the sculptor, the architect or planner does not attempt to create an object that will endure unchanged through time. A painting, photograph, or a ceramic vase represent final solutions. One cannot improve on a Van Gogh painting by adding to it or by changing the colors. The owner preserves it under conditions that will minimize change, and he will restore the painting if it is damaged. Individual buildings can be preserved in deference to former occupants or to their designers; an entire city like Port Townsend, Washington, can be an architectural museum. To convert a building or a city into a monument is to forge a link with the past. In contrast to monuments or museum pieces whose time milieu remains fixed, a design solution for a particular client's problem is an experiment. Insofar as it succeeds, it can be replicated and improved; but, since the client's needs, resources, and the available technology are always in flux, there is no final solution to a design problem. The time perspective of the designer must be diverted from rigidly-bound intervals and fixed timeless products to fluid and dynamic processes with myriad influences upon them.

The Darwinian revolution . . . is based on the concept that life is a process unfolding over vast spans of time. To formulate laws based on a static concept of time, such as "balance of nature," is to misconstrue the essence of the process. Natural selection—the force that shapes man and other existing forms of life—involves a dynamic change in which malleable organisms interact with a shifting environment. There are no stable elements in the system. Nowhere does the process sustain its existing forms. There is no balance. The scales are always tipping under new weights.[8]

One of the major contributions of James Hutton[9] to modern geology was his view of world as time. Writing that "waterdrops have worn the stones of Troy and swallowed up cities," he was able to perceive the power that rain might have over a thousand-year span. The fourth dimension of time altered his way of looking at water, wind, life, and death. A world without the experience of time is impoverished and lacks an essential quality of human experience. Through hypnosis one can experience a world without depth—a flat, drab, and lifeless plane. A world without time lacks an equally important dimension of human experience.

Some aspects of the ecological perspective have mystical connotations to laymen—time-as-flux is one of these. The meaning of this conception becomes clear when it is applied to a practical problem. First of all, any environmental change is likely to benefit certain individuals and institutions, to worsen the condition of others, and to force some to change, die, or move away. One of my students is currently studying the new pedestrian mall in Sacramento, California. Less than a year after the mall opened, some businesses evidently were helped by the absence of cars; others were seriously hurt. The mall was attracting its own clientele—pedestrian traffic, mothers and children enjoying the play areas, and older retired people on the benches watching the action. Although it is of practical interest to ask about the effects of the mall on existing stores, in the long run, this is an unimportant question. Over a period of years, the mall will attract its own clientele and its own stores suited to pedestrian activities.

Time is a major constituent of architectural experience. People's reactions to a building are influenced by the past, the present, and the future as well as by its physical dimensions, color, material, and style. A building can be programmed temporally as well as spatially to link the present with the past or the present with the future. A college library can emphasize the continuity of learning and the cumulative nature of scholarly research, as well as express the traditions of the academic community. The visitor to Oxford University is struck by the thought that 400 years earlier scholars walked down the same halls. One can design a newspaper office to enhance the here and now, the immediacy of the ephemeral present, disappearing as soon as it is portrayed in banner headlines. A scientific laboratory, bereft of familiar materials and forms, can challenge its occupants to imagine the world of tomorrow.

[8]Loren Eiseley, cited in Paul Fleischman, "Conservation: The Biological Fallacy," *Landscape*, 18 (2), 1969, pp. 23–26.

[9]Cited in Loren Eiseley, *The Firmament of Time* (New York: Atheneum Publishers, 1966), p. 25.

Prison designers have been admonished to pay particular attention to future trends because it is difficult to obtain funds to replace outmoded institutions. A community may outgrow its hospitals and schools and look forward to building new ones, but in the case of prisons and jails, the tendency has been to expand or to overcrowd existing buildings rather than to build new ones.[10]

The noted social psychologist Kurt Lewin[11] wrote, "The life-space of an individual includes his future, his present, and his past. Actions, emotions, and certainly his morale at any instant depend upon his total time perspective." Environmental experience is affected by such attributes as *duration*—the length of time one spends in a building or a city; *tempo*—how quickly people move or events pass (a lake looks very different at 70 miles an hour than it does while walking alongside it); *sequence*—certain routes will provide contrasts and surprises and make a building seem exciting and alive; *chronicity*—several brief visits will produce a different environmental experience than one long visit; and *familiarity*—the visitor and the old-time resident may share space but their experiences are different. Familiarity means orientation in time as well as in space—knowing how long it takes to get from one place to another, knowing that it takes 20 minutes to get to the airport, knowing whether it is a rush hour or a slack period. Studies of environmental perception cannot be based solely on casual visitors, although these "tourists" represent a valuable source of data to determine environmental experience before habituation has set in. Some of the most revealing comments about buildings may come from those people who are unable to adjust to them and depart, whereas some of the least informative may come from those who remain by "tuning out" or adapting to unsatisfying surroundings.

Socio-Cultural Time

Other cultures conceive of time in ways unfamiliar to most Westerners; these differences are often related to the structure of space. Indian psychiatrist Shashi K. Pande describes the Westerner's view of time as a "unique opportunity, to be utilized and be filled to the utmost with engagements, events, and endeavors in order to capture the richest share of life."[12] He

[10]R. D. Barnes, "Modern Prison Planning," in *Contemporary Corrections*, ed. Paul W. Tappen (New York: McGraw-Hill Book Company, 1951), p. 272.

[11]Kurt Lewin, "Time Perspective and Morale," in *Resolving Social Conflicts*. New York: Harper & Row, Publishers, 1948.

[12]Shashi K. Pande, "From Hurried Habitability to Heightened Habitability," *Proceedings of the First National Symposium on Habitability*, Los Angeles, May 11–14, 1970.

describes the visit of a Malayan prince who saw London for the first time when he attended the coronation of Edward VII in 1902. The prince remarked to his escort that he understood for the first time why Europeans valued time so highly: "In England each day is so packed with living that if a man misses so much as a quarter of an hour, never again will he catch up with the minutes which have escaped him. With us life saunters: here it gallops as if it were pursued by devils." In contrast to this is the profligate attitude of Western man toward space—he spreads himself around as if the earth were infinite. One wonders how the recent view of earth as a finite ball will affect the Western view of time. Perhaps the Westerner may loosen his grip on time—releasing experience from its temporal bonds—and enjoy the trip to the moon as well as the landing and splashdown.

The democratic ideal rejected the theory of historical causation and believed that the poor could rise out of slums, colonies could free themselves, and minorities could become integrated into the mainstream of society. Hard work would be rewarded and nothing was inevitable except death and taxes. History was a dry chronicle of past events, the names of victorious kings and queens, dates of wars and treaties, and the sites of battles and discoveries. There was no common thread running through the past nor any indication what form the future might take. It was a succession of events and individuals without a causal force. The American antipathy to long-term planning can thus be understood. Looking too far back denies our freedom of action; planning too far ahead will hinder the freedom of our grandchildren to determine their own present. As a rule of thumb, a man is supposed to plan for his children but not for his grandchildren— that is his children's job.

Psychiatrist Humphrey Osmond describes the Vietnam conflict as a war between two opposing forces with different time-space perspectives.[13] General Giap counts off the conflict in decades. He opposes the mighty American spaceman who, though he roams widely, is always short of time. The Americans are straining at the bit to "get it over with," and they complain that the war is "endless." One cannot foresee a quick solution to a war in which one opponent is committed to winning space while the other is trying to gain time. With their evolutionary view of events, Marxist theorists believe it is unrealistic to fix the status quo in a treaty or agreement since historical forces move by their own internal dynamics. It would be like passing a law that no acorn could become an oak or that snow could not become water. The only way to enforce such laws would be to destroy all acorns or to prevent them from coming in contact with the soil; or, in the case of snow, to keep it forever at a freezing temperature. In these cross-

[13]Comments contained in unpublished and highly-stimulating memoranda and letters, 1968–71.

cultural contacts, the effects of differences in time perspectives are most clearly felt.[14]

Perception can be defined as the interpretation of a stimulus, or as giving a stimulus a meaning; time concepts are intrinsic to this process. Consciously or unconsciously, all scenes are perceived in a time frame. There is an interaction between external cues and internal ones, and a relativity between one's own shifting time-coordinates and those of the outside world. All this has particular relevance for those who design or manage environmental settings. Blueprints, drawings, and photographs, even if they are three-D holograms, capture time at an instant and portray a static reality. Just as it takes a special act of consciousness to translate two-dimensional drawings into the mental image of a three-dimensional building, it takes similar mental effort, using somewhat different concepts, to add a fourth dimension of time to a three-dimensional building.

The sociologist Sorokin[15] maintains that each culture and academic discipline has its own conception of time—geological time with vast spans incomprehensible to most laymen, biological time based on rhythms and internal clocks, historical time based on events and cycles—and these differ in important ways from physico-mathematical time. Sorokin's particular concern is *socio-cultural time* which uses social events as points of reference and has these characteristics: (a) It does not flow evenly—one year in an urban society is packed with more changes than 50 years of existence in an isolated primitive tribe; (b) The appearance of markers and events is irregular—there are critical moments as well as dead time; (c) It is not infinitely divisible—one can rent a hotel room by the day or by the week but rarely for an hour or a minute; (d) It is determined by social conditions, and reflects the rhythms and pulsations of life in a given group. Within the same geographic area, different occupational and cultural groups will have different socio-cultural times. Every year Harvard University issues a calendar, which not only differs in important ways from the Harvard calendar of 50 years ago, but is vastly different from the calendar of workers in a local factory.

Socio-cultural time cannot be replaced by purely quantitative time without devitalizing it and making orientation in time virtually impossible. If all socio-cultural time conventions were removed—the beginning of the year, the week, the month, Christmas, special dates and holidays—we would be lost in time. There would be an unlimited number of units of mathematical time at our disposal—billions of seconds to use in measuring duration—but we would not know where to start and where to end. Mathe-

[14]E. T. Hall, *The Hidden Dimension*. Garden City, N.Y.: Doubleday & Company, Inc., 1966.

[15]P. A. Sorokin, *Socio-Cultural Causality, Space, Time*. New York: Russell and Russell, Publishers, 1964.

matical time is continuous and flows evenly, there are no physical dates or points of reference, the units are all identical and colorless, ignoring the qualitative aspects of time experience. By contrast, socio-cultural time contains markers and divisions which are sinful, holy, happy, times of harvest, times for sowing, for labor, and for rest, which in our experience are inseparable from time since they are tied in with the rhythms and pulsations of individual and group experience.

The same reasoning applies to *socio-cultural* space as distinct from physical-mathematical space. Notation systems for analyzing spatial experience are intrinsically bound with concepts of flow, duration, and periodicity.[16] Using these notations, a highway designer should be able to plan the experience of a driver or of a pedestrian just as a composer writes out a symphony as it will sound—not to the people who play it—but to the audience who hear it. Philip Thiel believes that skills similar to those of the composer or film editor will be required—a sense of rhythm, tempo, meter, and a feeling for the interrelationship of sequence.

Environmental experience does not flow evenly in equal time units—rather it begins and ends with certain events—entering a building, opening a door to one's apartment, leaving the apartment, leaving the building. The time worlds of different occupational groups in a single building are not likely to coincide. Secretaries and salesmen will have different time-coordinates—coffee breaks, lunch periods, and vacation times; different penalties for arriving late or leaving early, and different conceptions of how long each will remain at the same desk or at the same job. The physical structure of a building creates the distinction between inside and outside time. A secretary's day passes slowly when business is slack, but she anticipates an active social life in the evening. Her boss may be under extreme pressure to increase sales; there are not enough minutes in the day for him. Occasionally, to preserve his sanity, he dreams of the leisurely pace of his vacation when there is "nothing to do." The purpose of certain space dividers may be to keep people with different time-coordinates out of one another's way. Research scientists who operate without deadlines should not be mixed with technical poeple who must produce answers to fit the rhythms of the production line. Hospitals typically segregate the long-term or chronic patients from newly-admitted patients; and jails do the same for inmates.

Sometimes the objective of a building is to take a person out of one time and enclose him in another. An archeological museum moves a person

[16]See, for example, D. Appleyard, K. Lynch, and J. R. Myer, *The View from the Road.* Cambridge: MIT Press, 1964; or Philip Thiel, "Notes on the Description, Scaling, Notation, and Scoring of Some Perceptual and Cognitive Attributes of the Physical Environment," in *Environmental Psychology* (H. Proshansky, W. H. Ittelson, and Leanne G. Rivlin, eds.). New York: Holt, Rinehart and Winston, Inc., 1970.

The endless tunnels and funnels of the airport lead nowhere.

The passengers are out of place and out of time.

back centuries, whereas a science and technology museum projects him forward. A theater must be prepared to create and change time worlds rapidly. Resorts and retirement communities convey a freedom from outside time definitions. Good design means protecting the visitor against too abrupt a change in time worlds. The museum lobby may prepare the visitor for the shock of moving from the outside traffic into the Pleistocene era; the stodgy formality of a bank lobby slows the customer down to a dignified and un-hurried tempo.

There is a difference between a preserved historical building and the faked gimmickry of Disneyland. There is no comparison between the experi-ence of standing in awe in a redwood forest and realizing that these trees were in America before Columbus landed and of seeing a concrete replica of such a forest in Florida or in Los Angeles. One of the most important differences between the Disneyland building and the historical building is the time experience of the visitor—his ability to sense the continuity between the people who had actually lived in the building and himself, and his appreciation of what it meant to hew the timbers and fashion the nails by hand, and to bring the furniture around the Horn to San Francisco and transport it by land to the Pacific Northwest.

There has never been a more eloquent advocate of historical preserva-tion than John Ruskin:

> Do not let us talk then of restoration. The thing is a Lie from begin-ning to end. You may make a model of a building as you may of a corpse, and your model may have the shell of the old walls within it as your cast might have the skeleton. . . . But the old building is destroyed, and that more totally and mercilessly than if it had sunk into a heap of dust, or melted into a mass of clay. . . . We have no right whatever to touch build-ings of the past. They are not ours. They belong partly to those who built them, and partly to all generations of mankind who are to follow us.[17]

Geographer Wilbur Zelinsky[18] questions why two intervals between the ticks of a clock should be any more similar than two rectangular patches of land on a map. In the year 1800, Liverpool, Lima, and Tunis were at different levels of development, and each was stuck in its own time rut. Traveling from California to Kansas, one goes over one thousand miles east, and also goes back ten years in manners, morals, and symbols of popular culture.[19] Traveling across a small American city, there is a peeling

---

[17]John Ruskin, *The Seven Lamps of Architecture* (London: G. Allen 1904), pp. 185–186.

[18]Zelinsky, *op. cit.*

[19]The nineteenth-century German poet Heinrich Heine is alleged to have said, "If the world comes to an end, I shall go to Holland. There everything happens 50 years later."

back of layers of house styles and types from the new suburbs to the central city, and back again on the other side. Moving to another apartment is a time trip as one sorts through acquisitions and treasures, some of which have not been seen since the last move. There are high school yearbooks, old photograph albums, bundles of letters, tax receipts, unused wedding presents, and clothing which has been saved in the hope that the styles will come back. Decisions have to be made about what is to be saved intact, what is to be altered, and what is to be given away. Just as each man is his own reservoir of time, holding back immense quantities of experience, his possessions are layers from different periods of his life.

A room, a park, or a highway tells a visitor "Stay awhile" or "Get past me as quickly as possible." Duration messages apply not only to circulation areas but also to destinations. The poignant sign outside some motels and restaurants, announcing "This is the place," has a deep emotional significance. The intended message is that the traveler has driven all the way through *nowhere* and has finally arrived *somewhere*. He has reached the island in the sea, the oasis in the desert, the refuge in the wilderness. Too many buildings and public spaces lack a sense of place. A man drives on a freeway, which looks like any freeway, in a car, which looks like any car, and even the gas stations and motels are indistinguishable one from another. Airports are probably the ultimate of placelessness. The traveler parks his car, enters a vast funnel, walks through one tunnel into another, does not meet anyone, goes through a small doorway, sits down in a long tube, and perhaps does not even see the outside of the plane in which he flies. There is a slick sameness to airport shops—the Hertz and Avis girls in their neat uniforms, the insurance counters, the restaurants with identical menus, the newsstands, the souvenir counters with the sign, "What did you bring me?"[20]

According to J. B. Priestley, the air traveler exchanges time for space, and loses place in the bargain:

> Let us say that I travel by car, at 60 miles an hour, across the five miles of the Little Puddlefield District. I see a church, two farms, four bungalows, and an inn, successively within five minutes; I have a Time relation with this region. On the next occasion I fly over it in a jet plane on a clear day, look down and see all at once the church, the two farms, the four bungalows, the inn, and what was in Time is now in Space.[21]

The placeless environment means that more people will be spending more of their time in transit—never getting anywhere, never arriv-

[20]Robert Sommer, "The Lonely Airport Crowd," *Air Travel*, April, 1969, pp. 16–18.

[21]Priestley, *op. cit.*, p. 105.

ing.[22] The placeless enviroment resists all efforts at personalization; it does not change in response to user inputs, a man can leave his litter but not his mark. This homogenized setting tends to blur personal time relationships. The nowhere quality of the airport, the sense of being out of place, also means that the person is out of time. A well-designed building will give a person a sense that he is somewhere, not only to improve his orientation, but also to increase his feelings of personal relatedness to his surroundings, to enhance and legitimize the quality of his immediate experiences, and, to put it in plain language, to give him something to talk about afterward. Sequence and tempo are time-related concepts that must be included in the building program. An event will be affected by what preceded it and by what comes after it. The endless tunnels and funnels of an airport could be justified if they culminated in a grand panorama of openness and sky. One would feel exhilarated upon reaching the end of the last tunnel and finally stepping into open space. Instead one despondently finishes his journey strapped into a seat in a long narrow tube.

Hypnosis and Space-Time

Some of the most relevant data on the way time concepts are built into ordinary perceptions are found in research using hypnosis. The sense of time can be changed through specific instructions by the hypnotist to the subject. By means of hypnosis, a person can go forward and backward in time; the passage of time can be speeded up or slowed down; and individual items in a person's past can be temporarily obliterated or extended. Hypnotic regressions have been used diagnostically, to learn about repressed or forgotten memories, and therapeutically, to enable the individual to work out his difficulties in the time period in which they occurred. Aaronson[23] has undertaken a fascinating series of studies, in which he hypnoti-

[22]A good description of this attitude is found in the song "Goodbye and Hello" by Tim Buckley (© 1968 by THIRD STORY MUSIC, INC. All rights reserved):

> The velocity addicts explode on the highways
>   Ignoring the journey and moving so fast
> Their nerves fall apart and they gasp but can't breathe
>   They run from cops of the skeleton past
> Petrified by tradition in a nightmare they stagger
>   Into nowhere at all and then look up aghast
>   And I wave goodbye to speed
>   And smile hello to a rose

[23]B. S. Aaronson, "Distance, Depth, and Schizophrenia," *American Journal of Clinical Hypnosis*, 9, 1967, pp. 203–207; "Lilliput and Brobdignag—Self and World," *American Journal of Clinical Hypnosis*, 10, 1968, pp. 160–166; "Hypnotic Alterations of Space and Time," *International Journal of Parapsychology*, 10, 1968, pp. 5–36.

cally removed or expanded the past, present, and future, and changed the experience of depth, size, and distance. He found that removing depth produced withdrawal and irritability and also the sense of being hemmed in and separate from other people. Disturbances of gait were also evident. Increasing the experience of depth produced the feeling that objects and scenes were very beautiful; all subjects were exuberantly happy and compared the session to a psychedelic experience.

Reducing the size of objects produced feelings of anxiety and isolation. Each person sought methods of getting himself "back into scale" with his surroundings. One person solved this by reducing the scale of his own body through suggestion, and another, by imagining himself as a child. The subjects used similar scale-fitting devices when the world was increased in size. One reacted to the immense world with fear, but subsequently he fell asleep and dreamed he was standing in the nave of a large cathedral where he grew in size until he filled it completely. He awoke in tune with the world, as large as everything else, and at peace in a world in great magnificence.

Decreasing the subject's sense of distance produced profound pathological reactions in the first two subjects, and the investigator hesitated to use it any further. One man became afraid he would be attacked and hid all sharp and pointed objects from the experimenter. He accused people of stealing his air. The second subject felt that the walls were closing in on him and retired to his bed for the remainder of the session. He could be roused to activity only with great difficulty. Increasing the distance between the person and the world produced reactions of isolation and withdrawal, also quite distressing to the subjects. It is clear that the person's location in the world has profound implications for his self-concept—too little distance between himself and others is encroaching, too much is isolating.

It is an intriguing hypothesis that many of the behaviors observed in schizophrenia and other pathological states result from perceptual disturbances. Kinzel reported that prison inmates involved in frequent fights and aggressive incidents had relatively large bubbles of personal space and therefore needed more free space around them.[24] The autobiographies of mental patients show how supposedly bizarre behaviors make good sense if one understands how a patient perceives the world.[25] If people can't be trusted it may be prudent to withdraw and say nothing; if the world seems unreal, and all efforts to make contact result in failure, it makes sense to retreat and wait for things to improve. It is possible that the extreme sensory distortions found in some cases of schizophrenia also occur in varying degrees among the normal population and account for individual differences

[24]A. F. Kinzel, "Violent Persons More Afraid of Attack," *Hospital Tribune*, September 23, 1968.

[25]Robert Sommer and Humphrey Osmond, "Autobiographies of Former Mental Patients," *Journal of Mental Science*, 106, 1960, pp. 648–662.

in spatio-temporal worlds. An imposing entrance in a city hall may impress the middle-class business man, but it may frighten the welfare client.

Aaronson found that removing the subject's past through hypnosis produced confusion and disorientation. Expanding the past produced happy reminiscences and absorption in past events. Removing the present resulted in withdrawal and even immobility to a pathological degree. Expanding the present produced involvement and sensory enhancement. Objects and sounds became clear, luminous, and fascinating. Removing the future reduced anxiety since there was nothing to worry about and increased the person's interest in the immediate perceptual experience. These findings raise interesting questions about the most effective time frame to be used in solving a design problem. It could be argued that if we want designers to be absorbed in the world around them, it might be desirable to expand their awareness of the present and reduce thoughts about the future. This approach would be self-defeating since a planned structure is not a here-and-now enterprise but rather a future possibility to be used by people who either do not exist or who may change by the time the building is completed. The time frame of the designer must span buildings of the past and present, and how they work in practice, as well as be aware of the dialectical growth forces in society and the forms that these are likely to take.

Aaronson[26] has also studied the semantic connections between space and time. Depth was most clearly associated with time, width to a lesser extent, and height least of all. In three-dimensional space, past is located to the *back*, the *bottom*, and the *left*, future to the *front, top*, and *right*. Guilford[27] did a similar study and asked his students to make drawings to represent the past, present, and future. Most showed lines going from left to right, with the past below and the future above, and sometimes the present was pictured as the crest of a wave.

My colleague Charles Tart,[28] who is an accomplished hypnotist, undertook a small investigation of the connection between personal space and tempo. When people were told that their personal space bubbles had doubled in size, they walked very slowly around the room to avoid colliding with other people. When their space bubbles were reduced in size, people walked faster, since there was more free space in the room and therefore less risk of colliding with others. Expanding personal space to three times its normal size produced a euphoric reaction and a feeling of being protected. Expanding it to the size of the whole room generally dissolved the

[26]B. S. Aaronson, "Behavior and the Place Names of Time," *American Journal of Clinical Hypnosis*, 9, 1966, pp. 1–17.

[27]J. P. Guilford, "Spatial Symbols in the Apprehension of Time," *American Journal of Psychology*, 37, 1928, p. 420.

[28]Charles T. Tart, "The Hypnotic Investigation of Personal Space," unpublished manuscript, 1970.

effect, since personal space was no longer sensed. Retracting the boundaries of personal space to the individual's body had a dysphoric effect—people felt constricted, rigid, and unprotected.

In this chapter I have attempted to share what I have learned from my concern with time as an aspect of environmental experience. Some of the more salient points are:

1. Time is an inseparable ingredient of environmental experience. In the same way that we perceive color, texture, and shape, we perceive objects and situations in a time frame.

2. A building can be programmed temporally as well as spatially. A good designer aims at including certain time experiences in his building and at excluding others.

3. Many programs involving long-range planning have foundered upon the Western view of time as a short-run commodity. Frequently the time-coordinates dictated by existing political processes do not coincide with long-range planning needs.

4. Design education has overemphasized both the past and the future— the historical buildings of antiquity and the utopias of the future—at the expense of the present. Serious evaluation of existing buildings will provide valuable guidelines for designing new ones.

PART TWO

Evaluation

We don't have to start from scratch each year.

We've been making the same basic VW for so long now, you'd think we'd be bored with the whole thing.

But the fact is, we're still learning.

For no matter how perfect we think one year's model is, there's always an engineer who wants to make it more perfect.

You see, at the Volkswagen factory we spend 100% of our time making our car

work better and 0% making it look better.

Any change is an improvement.

And when we do make new parts we try to make them fit older models. So there's nothing to stop a Volkswagen from running forever.

(Which may explain why Volkswagens are worth so much at trade-in time.)

Starting from scratch each year can

get in the way of all that.

Just when they've ironed out the kinks in the current model, they have to face the kinks in the next.

We'll never understand all the hoopla over the "big changes" for next year's models.

 Weren't they proud of this year's?

CHAPTER SEVEN

The Volkswagen Model

Dear Playboy, . . . I'll be damned if I can find out how long the average *sexual act lasts, not counting foreplay. Give me a break with some kind of norm, will you, so I'll know how I'm doing? L. L. Birmingham, Michigan.*

The best way to find out how you're doing is to ask the person you're doing it with.—THE PLAYBOY ADVISOR. Playboy, *May, 1969, page 60*

Evaluation is tied up with notions like good or bad, desirable or undesirable, helpful or harmful. Any design question becomes first a value question—Which goals are to be achieved?—and secondly a political question —*Whose* values are to be served? Relationships exist between designers and clients (often a board or other corporate entity) who act as agents for a structure that will be occupied by another group, the consumers. This is especially true in institutions and public buildings such as schools, hospitals, airports, and housing for the elderly. To use sociologist Edgar Friedenberg's analogy we can say that institutional architecture is like the pet food business—the consumer is not the purchaser and unless the consumer becomes ill or bites the purchaser, there isn't going to be much change.

Criteria of user-satisfaction can exist alongside, yet need not replace, personal taste, expert opinion, and fashion, on the one hand, and structural integrity and perceptual values on the other. I do not imply that user-values have been totally omitted from the design process up to now, but rather that they have been used in an arbitrary, unsystematic, and often irrational manner. Frequently they are generated from an unrepresentative or inadequate sampling of people who are not themselves users of the particular type of facility but only agents of the users, such as a local housing authority, school board, or government agency. In this section I want to develop a model for generating user-inputs, feeding them into the design system, and institutionalizing the means for doing this. A word like *institution-alizing* is cumbersome and suggests a bureaucratic mechanism run by face-less clerks or by a computer. This need not be the case; the more self-conscious we are about the process, the less likely it will be for it to become bureaucratic.

User-inputs can be generated at any stage of the design process. During the planning stage, market research can be used to determine what the customers want. Ideally the designer has access to the consumers directly and will be able to ask them what they want as well as observe how they live at present. Part of his task might be to acquaint the potential consum-ers with the various options available, some of which they may never have experienced and which therefore may necessitate some simulation proce-dure. The designer would also have access to case studies or evaluations of similar projects elsewhere. None of these provides an infallible guide to the form the project must take, since this involves a creative synthesis of cost, siting, local ordinances, and a thousand other considerations.

When a project is completed it is possible to think of user-inputs in two senses. The first involves the structure as a servomechanical system which adjusts to changing user-inputs monitored through strategically-located sensing devices.[1] The client makes known his temperature needs by adjust-ing a thermostat which delivers the desired amount of heat or cool air to his immediate area. This sort of feedback loop does not include the architect and, once installed, becomes the responsibility of the maintenance engineer. The second sort of user-input involves direct dialogue between users and designers. A major impediment to such dialogue is the absence of the de-signer once the building is in use. Institutional means are necessary to bring the designer to the building periodically and put him in direct contact with users. Some defects or problems in the structure would be irremediable once finished, due to cost or other circumstances; follow-ups would be frustrating, but at least they could prevent such mistakes from being re-peated. However, few clients are willing to pay for evaluations that would benefit a third party at some future time, and the architect depends upon a fee structure to maintain himself and his office. Some new role must be found for the architect during this evaluation stage which gives him a rea-son (and a fee) for being there.

My feeling is that the role of *environmental consultant* is worthy of consideration. When a man buys a three-thousand-dollar car or a three-hundred-dollar refrigerator, he gets a book of instructions showing how to use it, describing all the features it contains, and listing the additional options available; when a school board receives title to a three-million-

---

[1]Raymond G. Studer, "On Environmental Programming," *Arena,* May, 1966.

dollar building, it receives little in the way of instructions how to make optimal use of the various features of the building. When I moved into a new tract house, it took four frustrating years of slamming the glass door back into the frame, forcing the lock up, requesting two visits from the door service people, and purchasing a replacement lock before I discovered a simple unmarked adjustment for regulating the locking mechanism. The same was true of the screen doors. I could not get them to stay on the runners, until one day, more than five years after moving into the house, I discovered little screws on the bottom that regulated the height of the runner wheels. I have seen instances where teachers responded to an open plan school by placing as many barriers as they could (bookcases, activity drawers, partitions) between individual areas. A teacher may not be aware of the possibilities that carpeting creates for working on the floor rather than at tables. An airport manager may assume that all patrons want to sit facing the runways and arrange his chairs in straight rows facing in one direction, creating an extremely unsociable environment and inhibiting all conversation between airport patrons. I have no doubt that a sensitive and intuitive architect can justify a per diem consulting fee by helping users and their agents get their money's worth from a new building. An additional bonus for the designer is learning how the structure works in practice.

Models already exist for professionals who render periodic service to clients over a several year time span. It is common for a patient to return for a checkup following major surgery; this may become routinized into annual visits or a "full physical," where the goal is not so much to ascertain the outcome of the last operation, but to catch present problems before they become serious. Many dentists send out reminders that six months have elapsed since the patient's last appointment. When a man buys a new car he is given a book of coupons which he redeems for inspections and maintenance services after he has driven a fixed number of miles. The difference between architecture and other professions is that the product is generally stationary. The client cannot visit the professional, so the professional must visit the site. The client would be buying a professional space consultation service; the focus would not be upon the building in isolation, but upon the connection between the structure and the client's day-to-day activities.

Evaluation must occur after the building has been in use for some time. It is illogical to differentiate between subjective ratings of comfort, aesthetic appeal, and efficiency, on the one hand, and "objective" measures such as illumination, temperature, and humidity, on the other. The temperature of the building, its humidity, and illumination are dependent upon the way the building is used. A classroom that is satisfactory for 20 children may be stuffy and hot for 30 children. The experiences of two Canadian building researchers who evaluated several test homes is instructive:

An attempt to compare the summer comfort conditions in two occupied houses of widely different construction failed because the differences attributable to the houses themselves were effectively masked by the uncontrolled opening and closing of windows. In another case two houses were fitted with aluminum windows and frames on an experimental basis and were to be observed over one winter. The tenants in one house reported no difficulty with the windows. They did, however, ventilate the house extensively by opening windows, and drying all washing outdoors, so that the indoor humidity in winter was so low as to cause no condensation on the aluminum frames. The tenants in the second house said the windows were satisfactory but on examination after a period of cold weather a coating of as much as one inch of ice had accumulated on the warm side of the window sills, a condition that would have been quite unacceptable to many tenants. These tenants never opened windows in winter and dried wash indoors, thus maintaining a high moisture condition in the house.[2]

The Volkswagen

When an architectural firm takes on a building type that it has never handled before, it is likely that there will be some flaws in the design. No one expects architects to be supermen. When architects make mistakes, the least they can do is *learn* from them. Furthermore the learning process should be empirical, shareable, and institutionalized within a communication system for the design professions. It is not enough that an architect learns from his own mistakes; the profession at large should learn something from them also. One can excuse a noisy or inadequate high school library, but not a third library no better than the first, or a twentieth no better than the third. Let us consider the concept of the flexible school building. This project involves a building shell whose internal dimensions could be altered quickly to form rooms or areas of many sizes and shapes.[3] Although the idea is good, I object to the fact that 30 schools like this were built without an evaluation of the model in practice. The design team for the flexible school had dissolved before the first school built along these lines opened its doors. It would have been more logical to open up three schools the first year, evaluate them, and embody the improvements in the five built the following year, and the 10 or 15 built in subsequent years.

[2]G. O. Handegord and N. B. Hutcheon, "The Use of Test Buildings in Building Research." Technical paper No. 104, Division of Building Research, Ottawa, Canada, 1960.

[3]Educational Facilities Laboratories, *SCSD: An Interim Report*. New York: Educational Facilities Laboratories, 1965.

Deficiencies observed in the first models should have been remedied in subsequent buildings.

The model of incremental improvements from one unit to the next should guarantee that each unit will be superior to its predecessor in user-satisfaction. Eventually one can develop a motel or college gymnasium "without bugs in it" and one "that works for the people inside."[4] Although I consider this a definite improvement over existing intuitive and pre-empirical design methods which make little or no systematic use of inputs from existing systems, the model is subject to the legitimate criticism that it is essentially closed. When one improves a Volkswagen, he has a better Volkswagen; and if he improves it enough, it becomes an excellent Volkswagen. As user-inputs change through technological developments or new patterns of living, it may not be possible to modify existing forms to meet new demands. Sometimes it is possible—the Volkswagen people superimposed a sports body on their little bug to make the Karmann Ghia, which, although it isn't a Porsche or BMW, is a sporty bug. When users wanted a larger sedan and a station wagon, the Volkswagen people ceased modifying the basic bug and used a new form. This reveals a crucial phase in the present evaluational model. Users and potential users must be asked about *overall* performance of existing or simulated units. We must know not only whether the ventilation, acoustics, lighting, chairs, and desks of a school are satisfactory; we also need to ask whether we need a school at all. Are prisons giving us the results we want, or do we need a new sort of institution? We are talking about *social architecture*, the design of social systems, as well as physical architecture.

In 1970, the editors of *Consumer Reports* gave the Volkswagen lower ratings than they had in 1967. They explained that the VW's performance had remained roughly the same over the intervening period, although there were several minor improvements, and that the competition had improved considerably during this period. Access to a data bank of evaluation does not mean stopping at page 1 or at the first "bug without bugs" but it means finding the best system for one's needs. The designer who has a bank of information available on existing, simulated, and prototype facilities should be able to devote himself more fully to programming and social architecture. Whatever emerges from his efforts will be subject to the same simulation, prototype, and evaluation procedures we have described. There will be ample room for novel pilot programs, institutions, and buildings, and these will be evaluated as integral parts of a continuous design and redesign

---

[4]The need to take local conditions into account makes the idea of a gymnasium or motel "without bugs" an unrealizable dream for practical purposes. One must still include sufficient flexibility and room for personalization in the design so that users can adapt the building to changed conditions.

process. When an architect develops a concept of a "bedroom hospital" or a buildingless airport where people drive directly to their planes, he cannot simply publish his ideas in the architectural press, receive acclaim from the mass media, and then move on to other exciting projects and leave his readers wondering how the idea worked out in practice. The developer of a new physical and social form is involved in its implementation, evaluation, and redesign. The architect's social responsibility is more than abstract concern for ghetto problems or the population explosion—it must include personal concern for the needs of the people affected by his buildings.

The lack of evaluational data not only causes the neglect of good design features and encourages an attitude of novelty for its own sake, since no one knows what items are good or bad, but it also results in the perpetuation of bad design solutions. Reinventing the wheel for each problem is bad enough, but reinventing a square or lopsided wheel is even worse. It is in the institutional field—the construction of schools, hospitals, post offices, and airports—where one finds the most flagrant examples of successive replications of bad solutions. The susceptibility of institutions to obsolete design lies in the lack of responsiveness of both designers and client representatives to user-inputs. Since they have a captive market, they are not concerned about loss of customers or even about consumer resentment unless it is organized politically. Schools get built and furnished according to stereotypes and traditions of the way schools are supposed to look. Prison design is probably most insulated from user-inputs, and the outcome is predictable. The handbook on prison construction published by the Bureau of Prisons declares candidly:

> Building committees, architects, and engineers, charged with (planning a prison), have had little to guide them beyond the catalogs and promotional talks of prison equipment companies, or, perhaps, a superficial knowledge—usually recently acquired—of similar institutions in other localities, which are themselves all too often based on archaic conceptions of prison planning. . . . The result is that the same traditional patterns of prison layout and design have been followed from state to state without stopping to consider wherein these concepts fall short of the best knowledge and practice available.[5]

In this case, evaluational data would *not* be a tool for insuring conformity, but rather they would point the way to departures from existing prisons. The lack of evaluational data has two unfortunate consequences—good features of existing prisons will be overlooked in the design of new ones, and bad features tend to be perpetuated out of ignorance.

[5]U.S. Bureau of Prisons, *Handbook of Correctional Design and Construction* (Washington: Bureau of Prisons, 1949), p. 6.

Nor will this approach inevitably produce a homogenized environment. I am sympathetic to the franchise distributors who have a financial stake in getting the bugs out of their products before they are distributed. A person who wants to open a Holiday Inn or a Colonel Sanders outlet knows that the franchise components have been use-tested and are compatible. This is a great advantage over ordering single items from a catalogue or from a contractor's specifications. What is wrong with so many franchise operations is that they have retail outlets as well as products which are tasteless and at variance with their surroundings. One drives through identical franchise strips in Omaha, Atlanta, and Los Angeles. This sameness in exterior appearance or in internal operation is not inherent in a systems approach. The team that developed the flexible school system made it explicit that individual schools could have virtually any exterior material they wanted—flagstone, brick, or natural wood siding. A motel system can provide that individual operators choose materials and graphics that blend into their local landscapes. There is no reason why a systems approach requires all buildings of a genre to look alike from the outside or the inside. Technically we can have the reliability and economics of use-tested products as well as the personalization and regionalization of design. Distributors of many franchise systems believe that it is financially advantageous to have all their buildings look alike—the customers will be looking for a golden arch or a rotating picture of the Colonel or the green Holiday Inn sign. Raising the design consciousness of the population may eventually prove to the distributors that buildings which fit or even raise the standard of local tastes and sensibilities are more profitable in the long run. The evaluation model does *not* make a homogenized environment inevitable. When the designer and his clients are freed from reinventing the wheel on every job and attending to the thousands of details and minutiae, they can devote more attention to external appearance, siting, and interior decor.

The model we have discussed can be applied irrespective of scale, providing the product is replicable. Often there is an inverse connection between social importance and evaluation—the larger and more fundamental the change, the less evaluation ensues. People who pioneer innovative systems or programs may be so busy keeping them going that they have no time for evaluation, or perhaps they may be temperamentally antagonistic to it. Two examples of nonevaluated innovations are open-plan schools and office landscaping. Hopefully this deficiency will be remedied in the next few years, but, for the moment, the writer has yet to see a systematic and thorough evaluation of either. Each has its dedicated prophets, acolytes, and propagandists, complete with glossy brochures, slogans, persuasive ideologies, and consulting services. All that is lacking is knowledge of how they work in practice. One could easily compile a list of 50 articles about office landscaping and perhaps 200 about open-plan schools, but they are almost unanimously pegged at the level of fashion commentary. Walls appear, disappear, fold, partition, or play peek-a-boo, just as hemlines rise and fall. The lack of serious evaluation may doom a good innovation for the wrong reasons; i.e., the partitions in a flexible school system may not open properly, or the traditional wall-mounted telephone systems are not appropriate for open offices and result in a tangle of floor-level wires.

Contributions of the Behavioral Sciences

The techniques of science cannot prove that anything is good or bad, desirable or undesirable. These are questions of value rather than fact. The extension of life to age 120 may be regarded as undesirable by many people; the limitation of life (contraception) may be considered a boon to society. The scientific method can generate relevant data with which intelligent decisions can be made—if we know the probable results of several policies, we can decide which outcome accords best with our values. The methods of science, and here I refer specifically to evaluation procedures, also can help to define and rank people's values and compare the values of different social groups. It is a plausible delusion to equate knowledge with values. The load of the policy-maker is not necessarily lightened by knowledge of user-values. Knowing that there is a conflict between the desires of different users places a heavier burden on him than supposing that everyone wants the same thing or than projecting his own values on the participants. Yet this knowledge may enable him to plan more intelligently and to encompass the needs of diverse user groups in the design solution.

Beginning with Freud, the behavioral sciences showed promise that knowledge of human drives and instincts could form the basis of a society which would permit maximum expression of impulses within the context of the general good. Unfortunately, the fact that a drive was part of man's genetic endowment proved a less than infallible guide to how and when people wanted it expressed. Stated in Freudian terms, knowing the id still left us ignorant about the ego and superego. Modern psychology has shown that human instincts are remarkably malleable; all people need nourishment, but they eat different things at different times in different ways. The study of this learning process—the ways in which behaviors are shaped by the environment—constitutes a second contribution of the social sciences. Knowledge of the learning process can help designers and space managers to teach people to use their environment productively and to keep abuse to a minimum.

There is a third contribution that the social sciences can make. We shift here from the deterministic and causal aspects of science, to application and technology. I refer to the methods in which social sciences *define* values, wishes, manners, and morals. With a few tools from my (hypothetical) Sears, Roebuck Social Science Kit—my handy questionnaire, my trusty interview guide, and my natural observation telescope—I can learn what people want, or discover what they do in a situation involving alternative choices. These techniques can form the basis of an evaluational model for environmental systems involving user-inputs.

In closing this chapter, I want to discourage the tendency to flagellate architects simply because they are accessible. Although they can be criticized for some of the ugliness and brutality, I would accuse them of being responsible for only a very small part of it; the good things they have done undoubtedly outweigh the bad. Their sins are those of omission rather than commission. The preceding remarks about neglect of users were intended less as an indictment for past misdeeds than as a stimulus to acquire new techniques, a new rationale, a new *raison d'être*, and new allies. The architect who designs for a jury of his peers will have little to inspire his projects except artistic license and professional self-justification. Designing buildings for the people who will use them provides a moral justification for his work and will increase his bargaining power with the bureaucratic forces.

CHAPTER EIGHT

Who Evaluates Buildings
and Who Pays the Cost?

The basis of knowledge about man's relationship to his environment is so flimsy, however, that architects will have to begin by feeling their way into problem statements and their desired results. This means that the crucial sixth step—evaluation—will have to be formalized and made a part of "normal" practice. Except for architectural criticism, there is not even any pretense at evaluation of completed projects within current practice.—JOHN EBERHARD

The question is frequently asked, Who should generate user-inputs—the psychologist, the designer, some new hybrid professional such as the architect-psychologist or sociologist-planner, or the users themselves? I don't believe it is necessary to answer this question now. Essentially it is an empirical question. In a few years' time we will know who is able to make sense out of buildings in use. The history of professions offers us the lesson that one profession cannot rely on another to evaluate its work. Architectural schools are currently hiring psychologists; large architectural offices will soon follow suit. Left to himself, the psychologist is likely to be irrelevant and ineffective in the design fields. Some form of team arrangement where he would be working with a group of design, engineering, systems, and subject matter people during the programming and evaluation stages is the alternative.

At the present time it is necessary to acquaint architects with behavioral research methods to develop greater sensitivity to user-behavior. Just as we need to develop the means to increase environmental awareness and to make people more knowledgeable about the possibilities inherent in their surroundings, we must also show architects the role of the consumer in selecting, adjusting to, and adapting his environment. The goal is not to make architects into junior-grade social scientists, but rather to fill an urgent need for a design-behavior middleman that is not met by existing training programs. It is unrealistic and unwise for social scientists to undertake evaluation and attempt to feed back the information to designers. This results only in irrelevant studies with conclusions that will be misunderstood and misapplied. On the other hand, it would be equally unrealistic to expect designers to become researchers. Although a designer should visit his buildings while they are in use and watch and talk to the occupants, the undertaking of systematic surveys requires a particular sort of temperament and set of skills. It is important that practitioners *know about* research even if they are not going to undertake research themselves. This should increase communication between architectural researchers, who will be feeding evaluational data to practitioners, and the practitioners, who will be implementing the researchers' findings. A few individuals will possess both design and research skills.

Who Pays the Cost?

There is also the legitimate question of who is going to pay for the evaluations. There are many answers to this question, but no single answer. Clients should help underwrite some of the cost in evaluation in return for the consultative services of the designer after the structure is completed and in use. A contract for a new building should include a minimum two-year follow-up consulting period in which the designer helps the client get his money's worth from the building and at the same time collects necessary evaluational information. Once it becomes clear that the building rather than the architect is being evaluated, this approach may generate considerable evaluational data. If the idea of postoccupancy consulting is realized, specialized firms may deal specifically with evaluation and consultation. At the moment there are several design firms that confine their efforts to programming; they secure user-inputs which they relay to the architect before he makes his drawings. Such a firm, which would already possess the necessary survey and rating skills, could expand its scope to include evaluation.

Major design contracts could include periodic evaluations by an outside agency specializing in such work. The agency might be a letterhead organization, without full-time staff, under the aegis of a university department of architecture or planning. It would contract on a per diem basis with interested faculty members in design and social sciences, as well as in specialty areas such as education when school facilities were involved, or health sciences when a hospital or clinic was involved. Consumer rating services maintain a roster of interested scientists and technologists who can be called upon for advice or assistance. Frequently these men are not named officially since they hold positions where their association with consumer testing service might provoke some controversy. Yet it seems reasonable that an evaluation service working on a hospital project might call on a local doctor or pharmacist for assistance. The use of outside consultants will require standardized rating scales using clearly defined categories.

The evaluation process might also be organized and supported by professional associations in a specific field. Museum directors might establish a standardized rating form as the basis of a data bank which would cover subjects such as humidity control, display cases, and outdoor exhibit areas. The system would be open-ended, capable of access from decentralized locations, and available to people who require the desired item only as a small part of an overall project. Presently an architect designing a science museum as part of a high school does not have the time or the facilities to adequately research display cases. He can find some pictures and descriptions of existing museums but little in the way of concrete data. With the trend toward professionalization, there is considerable potential for space managers, such as hospital administrators, school superintendents, and cafeteria directors, to organize evaluational data banks in their respective fields. The enterprise might be sparked and financed by a government agency: the Office of Education might do this for schools; the Department of Transportation· for highway interchanges or roadside parks; and the Department of Agriculture for housing for migrant workers.

Some of this work is being done. In 1969 there were at least three studies underway within a fifty-mile radius of migrant farm housing—each investigator was working independently of the others and there was virtually no sharing of the results. The National Institute of Mental Health has supported studies of mental health centers and mental hospitals. These studies are closed systems, with different categories used to describe each structure, and they contain very little in the way of behavioral data. Private foundations might help an evaluation system to get started. The Ford Foundation, with its subsidiary, The Educational Facilities Laboratories, has made tentative beginnings in this field—but the information systems remain closed and essentially nonevaluative. Colleges, universities, and research institutes, with their large reservoir of captive labor and brainpower, could also initiate such an evaluational data bank. A required part of a design student's training would be to do an evaluation of an existing facility. This kind of project can bridge the gulf between the university and the outside world. Evaluation projects on the scale necessary will require a tremendous expenditure of energy and effort, not easily supplied by professional architects and social scientists. The only group large enough and sufficiently motivated to undertake an immediate crash program of evaluation are students in the various design and environmental fields.

Evaluations might also be sponsored by manufacturers' trade associations or by consumer groups. Considering the competitive nature of the commercial world, however, it does not seem a likely place to look for objective evaluation of products. Organizations like Consumers Union do not ordinarily look at systems on the scale of an airport, post office, or public housing project, yet one can imagine some sort of urban group, interested in environmental quality, which would attempt to generate a data bank about city parks or about municipal buildings.

Some people are extremely pessimistic about relying on existing agencies to develop a data bank of architectural evaluation. Grady Clay, the editor of *Landscape Architecture*, was moved to ask:

> What sorts of surveillance, critical evaluation, and criticism can we expect from present institutions involved in changing the physical environment? The federal government? Why expect it to produce effective criticism of its own projects? The Budget Bureau shows no concern for anything other than old fashioned economy. The U.S. Department of Urban Development has come up with no reliable system of public review for its billions of dollars worth of new environment. Nor have other huge developers, the Departments of Agriculture, Interior, Commerce, or Defense. . . . Should we expect much from existing professional societies? They show little inclination at the moment to police the quality of their members' work. Rules of professional conduct within A.I.A., A.S.L.A., A.I.P., and A.S.C.E. prohibit or discourage members from making a public critique of a fellow member's work.[1]

Similar pessimism is voiced by a critic of the New York City subway system. Observing that traffic and transit problems in New York City are handled in the manner of a doctor who treats an ailment without querying the passenger about side effects, she also objects to the idea that the public pulse can be taken by the transit authority which is "incapable of coming up with a good procedure, let alone a fair result. . . ." The writer is equally pessimistic about a new Office of Transportation whose "studies" amount to a reshuffling of the same tired old studies completed by previous departments. Since the city government is not offering effective evaluation, the writer recommends that subway and bus riders should band together for their own protection and should do their own evaluation.[2] This prospect is likely in situations where commercial firms, government agencies, and professional societies do not respond to users. If established groups do not evaluate public housing, schools, and hospitals, organized consumers are going to do it themselves—in many cases, more heat than light will be the inevitable result. I hope that professional societies, government agencies, or industry groups specializing in particular building types will begin serious

[1]Grady Clay, "Who Says 'Never Look Back'?" *Landscape Architecture*, January, 1968, p. 111.

[2]Carol Greitzer, "The Confusing Logistics of the New York Subway," *The Village Voice*, August 10, 1967, p. 6.

evaluations and will make knowledge and improvements cumulative before the critical point is reached when users do this job for them. In order to be a professional there must be *continuous* evaluation of one's work. A professional does not provide a service without devoting some effort to finding out whether the service meets the client's needs. This is different from the attitude of a nonprofessional group of manufacturers who rely on public acceptance of a product as the test of its worth. Professions such as law, medicine, and architecture have been granted monopolies and privileges by the government; in return, members of these professions are expected to be responsive to the needs of society.

Such an evaluation bank is both necessary and inevitable; once established, it could conceivably be self-sustaining and even profitable. One can foresee a subscription service in the field of school design or in hospital construction that would disseminate information to clients for an annual fee or for a retrieval fee per item. No architectural office that wanted to keep up with current trends could afford to be without access to such an information system.

User Self-Surveys

If the goal is to secure reliable evaluations which will go into a central data bank, any one of a number of different groups can initiate and sponsor this. If the objective is to change someone's behavior, however, that particular person must be involved in the evaluations from the outset. Hit-and-run evaluations of a hospital by a team of outside experts are not likely to change the attitudes and policies of the hospital board unless they have been intimately involved in the survey from the outset. Since people already have defenses built up against listening to unfavorable information, few results can be expected from a team that appears one day to take a survey, disappears, and submits a report six months later. There is a difference between information for a central data pool which *can* be gathered by an outside team of experts on a hit-and-run basis and information that is likely to change the opinions and policies of the person surveyed.

Let me offer a personal illustration: There are a number of rating scales for mental hospital wards which I could use at any of the nearby mental hospitals. However, if I were to contact a local mental hospital, conduct a survey of their wards, and then send them a report telling them my opinions about the color scheme they were using, the comfort of the furniture and the beds, access to the outside, adequacy of the toilet facilities, and so forth, I am quite certain that I would get a cordial thank-you note from the superintendent and that that would be the end of it. Even if I wrote an article about hospital environment, it would not be likely to change the attitudes or behavior of the people whose wards were surveyed. The only way to change their policies would be first of all to convince them that ward design is important and then to encourage them to ask how things can be improved. We might then *jointly* undertake a survey to find out how patients and staff feel about the present facilities. I would have several questionnaires available in my briefcase, but I would ask them to supply some items themselves. It is important that they have a role in composing the interview form. There is a very useful compromise between standard items that would be useful for a central data pool and local items. Questions about storage space and bathroom facilities and dining areas will probably be useful in many situations, but there will be more specific local issues that should also be covered—this is a good focus for local involvement in drawing up a survey form. The next step is to persuade the patients and staff to *carry out the survey themselves.* This is exceedingly important. Certainly it would be easier for me to compose the questionnaire myself and to pay a graduate student to carry it out. The involvement of the people themselves in the questions and answers is essential at every stage, however, if opinions and policies are going to be influenced in any significant way.

The next step, which is often overlooked but should not be, is to make a pilot test of the research instruments. No matter how competent and careful the question makers have been, there are always items which are ambiguous or confusing to the respondents. It is absolutely essential to try out the instruments, discuss the person's answers with him afterwards, and check the reliability of the observation categories. This can also be used as a means of training the interviewers or observers. It is likely that some modifications will be made in the length or content of the instrument on the basis of the pilot study.

When the survey is completed, the people involved tabulate the results themselves. With questionnaires or observation sheets, no fancy statistics are necessary. Usually it is sufficient to calculate the percentage of people who are satisfied with each particular item and the percentage who have complaints. With open-ended questions where the respondents are likely to ramble, the scoring is a bit more complicated. Some sort of *content analysis* must be used—skimming over the responses and picking out the major categories and then tabulating their frequency. I have always considered it important to let people tabulate the responses themselves—to make up totals in each category—before I see the results. It is likely that they have made some mistakes in analysis and tabulations, such as combining the replies from two categories that don't belong together or forgetting to total the "no answer" replies. I meet with the tabulation team, indicate how the analysis might be improved, and then let them do a reanalysis of the questionnaires. When this is finished a meeting is held with all the people concerned with the ward—patients and staff alike—to go over the survey

results. There are usually three stages to this session: first, the survey results are described; second, they are interpreted and considered by all those
present; and, finally, the participants discuss action to improve the situation. This discussion should go beyond criticism to suggestions for positive
action. In the most successful cases, local people organize or take concrete
steps to solve the problems that were revealed by the survey.

The role I have outlined for a social scientist is similar to that of the
advocate architect, advocate planner, or advocate artist. It requires pa-
tience, a feeling for people, an ability to listen, and a willingness to talk
with people on their own terms. One measure of the success of a community
self-survey is the extent to which it influences community attitudes and
policies.

From the standpoint of research, however, there is much to be said for
the team of outside experts brought in for a definite period to undertake a
specific survey or series of observations. The study of new office buildings
in London which was commissioned by the Ministry of Technology is a
good example of this kind of survey.[3] The results from several thousand
offices are put together to get an overall picture of the office situation. These
results are not likely to change the policies of the offices surveyed. Each
approach has its own objectives. If one's goal is to change an existing situation—to improve it so that it becomes more satisfying to the local people,
—the community self-survey and the advocate social scientist and designer
are called for. But if one's goal is to generate reliable data that will be useful in designing new facilities, the outside evaluation team is preferable.

An evaluation bank should include both technical measures and user-
reports. A description of a hospital should include technical information
about heating and the structural qualities of the walls as well as the reactions of nurses and patients. When technical data conflict with user-reac-
tions, the answer may be a higher order explanation that encompasses
both sets of facts. The answer to a problem may be that the cooling system
is not being maintained properly, that it was installed in the wrong way,
or that local conditions require its alteration. There is no substitute for
evaluation in the field to augment research in the laboratory. The possibility that a building may not be being used properly—the internal partitions interfering with the air circulating system, or a heavy work load in an
area planned for low density—is one reason for bringing technical experts
into field evaluations. Assigning the evaluation of buildings or cities to
people who are technically competent in interviewing and survey procedures, but who know nothing about the technical end of the project, is not
desirable.

[3]F. J. Langdon, *Modern Offices*, National Building Study Research Paper 41,
HMSO, 1966.

Ideally there is an evaluation team that includes a designer, a subject matter specialist (someone knowledgeable about libraries if a library is being evaluated or about hospitals if it is a hospital project), and a member who is competent in social science methods and approaches. If I had to settle for a single individual to make an evaluation I would choose someone trained in design with a strong user-orientation. Since the new generation of design students are people-oriented, such an individual will not be too hard to find in the coming years. For a two-man team, I would choose a designer with a behavioral orientation and a social scientist knowledgeable about the subject area (hospitals, schools, factories, or public housing). If it were possible to add a third team member, I would choose a subject matter specialist knowledgeable about developments in the particular field; the fourth member would probably be a people-oriented engineer. An evaluation team larger than five or six members would not be feasible— both from the standpoint of economics and from that of good working relationships.[4] If there are less than six or seven individuals on the team, the ability of the members to work together is most important. Being able to mesh one's own contribution with that of other professionals takes time, effort, and above all, a capacity to listen and exchange ideas. Often it seems that the drawbacks to teamwork—the tedious, confusing, and frustrating airing of different goals and jargons; the discussion of narrow versus broad conceptions of purpose; and interpersonal friction—outweigh the benefits of pooling the contributions of diverse specialists. Some technical experts, psychologists as well as engineers, do not know how to communicate with people outside their own specialty. These are not the sort of people to put on an evaluation team.

[4]My most fruitful team effort involved the programming of a resort complex in the Fiji Islands. The team included two architects, an engineer, a city planner, an artist (graphics specialist), and myself. Our good working relationships were abetted by the two days we spent slogging around the island getting to know the terrain and one another.

CHAPTER NINE

A Data Bank for
Design Information

*Why are so many of the new playgrounds stagnant? And
why are so many expensive mistakes made over and over again?
One reason may be that there is no central body whose job it is
to collect experience and research throughout the world, digest
it, and make it readily available to architects and planners.—*
LADY ALLEN OF HURTWOOD

One may foresee changes in architectural information systems coin-
ciding with improvement of evaluation methods. There will be movement
toward the format of a technical journal and away from the fashion magazine. The architectural press may even initiate a policy that no building can
be described or evaluated until it has been in use six months or longer.
Ego problems as well as ethical considerations will be raised when it comes
to identifying designers, clients, and consumers. John Eberhard believes
that the lack of evaluation is caused at least in part by the code of ethics
of the American Institute of Architects, which implies that no architect
should make derogatory comments about another's work.[1]

Fortunately some useable models exist in other fields. It is the general
rule in the social sciences that the confidentiality of the interviewee be protected—the same procedure can work in the design fields. The evaluation
and photographs of the building could be published, but there need be no
specific mention of the name of the client or designer. Such a procedure
emphasizes that a building rather than a firm is being evaluated. This seems
congruent with developments in the design fields where individual responsibility is gradually being eroded. In a large architectural office one is likely
to find buildings passed from one team to another. No one feels particularly

[1]John P. Eberhard, interview in *Engineering News-Record*, May 8, 1969, p. 25.

102

responsible, since each person knows that his opportunity to influence the final product is severely limited. Occasionally one finds a building in which budget limitations, local ordinances, or client instructions have altered the original design so substantially that the architect disavows responsibility for the final product. Even when a single architect undertakes a job from start to finish, his solutions may be so influenced by outside factors that his primary job is to juggle constraints and to arrive at the best possible compromise. These unfortunate aspects reinforce the idea that one should evaluate buildings or even more correctly, man-environment systems, rather than designers.

My colleague Nancy Russo, whose opinion I respect greatly, feels that not identifying the designers is both idealistic and unrealistic. I accept the fact that people in the immediate vicinity of an evaluated building will know its identity; for them, the lack of identifying information is superfluous. However, designers in other cities, states, and countries will not know who designed a given structure or who owns it. They can read about a housing project for the elderly or about a post office and learn what works and what doesn't, without knowing the designer or even the specific location of the building. I realize that there could be some benefit in knowing the location and client, but it is out-weighed by the risk that listing names will make people reluctant to have their buildings evaluated. This sharing of design information will increase professional identity among the design community. The basis of professionalization is commitment to the welfare of the client and the community, even at the risk of foregoing short-range economic gain. The physician does not withhold information about a new operation that will save people's lives; the ethics of his profession require him to share this information with his colleagues.

A consumer rating approach which extolls particular products differs in several important respects from the evaluation bank we have been discussing. The objective of a consumer rating service is to compare brand-name products, whereas the evaluational model is oriented toward evolving new systems incorporating the best features of existing ones. By focusing upon one-shot successes or failures, the consumer rating approach draws attention away from the idea of cumulative small scale improvements to replicable design solutions. Such an approach would not offer much improvement over the status quo, except that awards might be more rationally assigned. Firm A would become known for its excellent school, awarded "Best Buy" in the 1977 issue of *School Evaluation Newsletter*, and school districts would seek to hire Firm A or would ask others to build its design.

Instead, there should be a nonproprietary bank of building evaluations without architects' names which could be used by any designer who feels they are applicable. The client relies on the professional dedication of the designer to do the best possible job. This means incorporating elements of successful solutions whenever possible, or designing a totally new system in the framework of other efforts which have applied the same principles. Except in those cases where a new material or technical process has been developed, most "totally new" design solutions have some precedent. I would seriously question the professional competence of a designer who could not benefit from the knowledge of how the design solution he proposes has worked in the past.

It would be a tactical error to begin the data bank in some highly-specialized or esoteric area. Although it might be interesting to examine a playground for spastic children or a garden designed for use by the blind or the Guggenheim Museum, the evaluations could not be generalized to other settings. Each of these places is so unique that it deserves to be looked at as an individual case study rather than as the forerunner of multiple replications. It would be better to begin the evelution bank with playgrounds, parks, schools, hospitals, or post offices. In time there is likely to be cross-referencing between evaluations of different building types using the pattern language approach.[2] Replicable elements, such as waiting rooms or child care areas, could then be combined to fit a particular design problem.

Since the institutional fields with close ties to governmental agencies have the strongest traditions in research and evaluation as well as available manpower to undertake systematic evaluation, the data bank would probably begin in the health, education, or social service fields. Its development is likely to be a matter of fits and starts, but if the emphasis is on cumulative knowledge rather than immediate application the long-range effect should be profound. Consumer rating services began by choosing products that their subscribers seemed most interested in, or for which the need for testing seemed to be most urgent, or for which tests were most readily available.[3] There seems no reason why environmental evaluations could not proceed in the same pragmatic way. As the amount of information in the system increases, the guidelines for future research and evaluation can be drawn according to a more inclusive and theoretically sound plan. The gaps in our knowledge should at that time become more evident, and the possibility of applying developments across building systems will be more feasible.

A number of computerized data archives are presently in operation covering everything from test scores of school children to economic growth in underdeveloped countries. Most of these data archives have policy committees which provide guidelines governing release of materials as well as

[2]Christopher Alexander, *et al., Houses Generated by Patterns.* Berkeley: Center for Environmental Structures, 1969.

[3]Helen Sorenson, *The Consumer Movement.* New York: Harper and Row, Publishers, 1941.

the acquisition of new data. Materials are generally supplied to outsiders on a cost-reimbursable basis in accordance with the computer and personnel time required to fill the request. Some data archives have technical facilities for preparing special analyses.[4]

The information bank will provide the basis for a more systematic kind of architectural research. The information bank would allow a researcher to sample building types and abstract the salient features of each for his project. I don't want to be unduly critical of the present emphasis on the case study approach. Given available resources, manpower, and tools, it is probably the most fruitful approach for a single investigator. The study of a Berkeley dormitory by van der Ryn and Silverstein was based on a single building at one period in time.[5] Given the state of the art, this proved an almost Herculean effort for the two young investigators and their team of graduate students. Within the next two or three decades the case study approach will give way to a more systematic and sophisticated approach to data storage about replicable building types as well as elements or patterns that cut across types. There is much to be said for a university maintaining the data bank of building evaluations. The students provide low cost manpower in return for valuable learning experiences. The time coordinates of the university are without rigid deadlines that would limit evaluations to six months or to a year; evaluations could continue through the life of the building using successive student evaluators. University departments could take full responsibility for evaluations and assure their credibility by involving faculty from the social sciences to work with field evaluators and help to collate the data.

In a recent issue of the *A.I.A Journal*, criminologist Norman Johnston makes a cogent plea for a data bank, including performance evaluations, for correctional architecture.

> A final suggestion—more limited and more specific: namely, that some sort of modest clearing house be set up so that the innovation and mistakes as well as the plans from one construction effort might become available to other correctional administrators and architects. The participants of this conference, for instance, have a tremendous accumulation of experience which somehow should be made available to others. The planning section of the Federal Bureau of Prisons has channelled many such requests and information in the past, but there now seems to be a need for a more formal arrangement. Correctional construction is taking place at an increasing pace. Although less extensively than in the past, architects are frequently sent to nearby states to inspect new prison structures. But

[4]L. F. Schoenfeldt, "Data Archives as Resources for Research, Instruction, and Policy Planning," *American Psychologist*, July, 1970, pp. 609–616.

[5]Sim van der Ryn and Murray Silverstein, *Dorms at Berkeley*. Berkeley: Center for Planning and Development Research, 1967.

there are financial limits on the distance which can be travelled and the number of institutions which can be seen. This problem becomes particularly serious when foreign countries, especially in underdeveloped areas, decide to embark on a program of construction. Representatives cannot easily be sent abroad but they are often anxious to learn of developments in America or Scandinavia or Britain. An inquiry came to me the other day from an Australian official whose government intends to build a treatment center for alcoholic prisoners. He wanted plans and details of any such institutions in the United States. Not so long ago an official of the French Ministry of Justice was anxious to learn of new jail construction here and in South America because of a planned expansion of detention facilities. The Director General of a South American prison system wanted plans for the new minimum security housing unit erected at Walla Walla, Washington. These requests and others like them represent a very sensible desire to profit from developments elsewhere, to avoid costly mistakes and to emulate successful innovations. If some kind of clearing house could be established on a small scale, with cooperation among state correctional departments, architectural firms, and foreign governments, the likelihood of financial savings and the prevention of unfortunate mistakes would seem considerable.

Plans and descriptions might initially be supplied, with some details of the success and failure of given features provided after a year or so of operation. Whether the proper location of such a clearing house would be in the Social Defense section of the United Nations Secretariat, in the Federal Bureau of Prisons, or in the A.I.A. itself, would be a matter for further exploration.[6]

As a well-known consultant on prison design, Johnston has found himself serving as a one-man clearing house for requests for information from state correctional departments, architectural firms, and foreign governments. Even with frequent consultations with penologists from around the world and visits to new correctional facilities, this role is impossible for one man to perform. The same is true in the design of airports, libraries, hospitals, or housing for the elderly. Institutional architecture can no longer rely upon the collective wisdom of competent practitioners transmitted in a haphazard, incomplete, and subjective manner. There needs to be a data bank of design information including building evaluations that is available to practitioners and clients alike.

The computer provides a means of storing vast quantities of data and retrieving it quickly. Although it may eventually form the basis of a design information bank, the present cost of retrieval may make it more feasible to begin the system with a central data storage center using loose-leaf evalua-

[6]Reprinted with permission from Norman B. Johnston, "Recent Solutions: The Criminologist's View," *A.I.A. Journal*, July, 1961.

tion sheets filled out by approved field workers under university auspices. These would be stored on microfilm and distributed via positive prints, using one of the newer copiers. Microfilm has definite advantages over the computer in regard to photographs and drawings. When a sufficient number of evaluations in a particular area became available, they could be duplicated and distributed in folio form. For the first few years, several clerks, under the supervision of a designer, could maintain such a data collection and distribution system. The system, which could be expanded as demand warranted, should not threaten the present basis of architectural practice in the United States. Rather it represents the highest hope of preserving a decentralized architectural system. If a firm in Spokane, Washington, is attached to an international data bank and, at the press of a few buttons, can obtain the specifications and evaluations of the latest hospitals, it can remain in the hospital design field. Otherwise there is great likelihood that the small firm will be squeezed out by a few large experienced hospital design firms or by large offices with special hospital design teams.

A book, even an excellent one such as *Planning for Play*[7] by Lady Allen of Hurtwood, is limited by being a closed system. Lady Allen, a sensitive and talented landscape architect, visited and photographed numerous playgrounds in England and on the Continent, and she presents them along with her evaluations. That is fine as far as it goes. But, if a practitioner later improves upon one of the designs she presents, the result will never reach the readers, who find the book as it was originally published. Like a photograph, a book records a reality at a particular time. The magazine article can bring recent news to a specialized audience. Coupled with abstract and reference services, it serves relatively well in the basic sciences. However, the back-up services include a virtual army of review, reference, and storage people. When an article is published about a new adrenalin derivative, the research has been done by scientists trained in research, familiar with the literature in the field, and with access to existing studies and knowledge of other people working on similar problems through their publications and face-to-face contacts at scientific meetings. The article will be read and evaluated by editorial reviewers competent in the field, published in a specialized journal known to contain articles in this area and received by scientific and scholarly libraries throughout the world, and abstracted by several journals in the field as well as interdisciplinary journals. The article will be cited in annual reviews of work on biochemistry and in the literature on adrenalin from that time forward, and the original experiment will be repeated and extended by numerous workers at other institutions. With these back-up services, a journal article can serve as a

[7]Lady Allen of Hurtwood, *Planning for Play*. Cambridge, Mass.: The M.I.T. Press, 1969.

reasonable means of communicating scientific information. However it, too, has drawbacks. For one thing the publication lag in many fields is unduly long and leading scientists rely more and more upon correspondence, face-to-face contacts at conferences, and mimeographed newsletters to report news of latest developments. Journal articles are severely limited in length and only the sketchiest information about the background of the work or the details of the procedure can be presented. Finally the number of journals published throughout the world as well as the interdisciplinary relevance of many discoveries means that for practical purposes no scientist is able to keep abreast of developments by reading the journals himself. He must rely on secondary sources, face-to-face contacts, and just plain luck to keep up with the latest work.

Journals devoted to specific topics such as school furnishings and airport construction exist at present, but these are more like trade magazines than scientific periodicals. They contain more gossip and fashion than substance. Articles describe new government programs, financing arrangements, buildings not yet constructed, use of materials without detailed evaluations, and contain virtually no cross-referencing to other studies and developments. Little effort is made to develop a cumulative and coherent body of current information.[8] Anyone who reads these journals looking for hard information concerning how an airport baggage system really works is going to be disappointed. If he is lucky enough to find an article on the topic, he will find some nice pictures, some frothy and superficial text, and quotes from airport directors and airline managers; but he will not find much in the way of hard data on the way the items work in practice or a detailed comparison of alternate methods of baggage handling. One reason for the dearth of information is the lack of research, but whatever research has been done tends to remain unknown and unread, buried in someone's files or in a library somewhere. Even when a firm has systematically evaluated five different baggage handling systems, the next firm programming an airport probably will have to do all this work over again.

Future designers will do less traveling and more reading. There is a pressing need for a new sort of information sharing system in the design fields. It may be possible for designers to go directly into computer storage and retrieval without establishing data-based journals first. If the Department of Transportation wanted to subsidize a data-based journal on airport

---

[8]An irate architect protested to me that the editor of an architectural journal had removed all the footnotes and references from his article. I can appreciate an editorial policy which puts emphasis on readability, but sooner or later the design professions will have to accept the cumulative nature of knowledge. Without footnotes, references, or citations to other studies, the reader has the impression that no one ever studied the topic before. It also makes it very difficult for someone interested in a problem to locate relevant studies.

construction—with problems ranging from noise and air pollution to wait-ing areas for children—this could be accomplished quickly using the format of the basic sciences. A small initial subsidy—a fraction of the cost of an airport in a medium sized city—could begin such a venture, or it could be started by the association of air terminal managers or some other manage-ment group. Whatever information system is developed should meet at least the following requirements:

1. It must be open-ended. New items of information can be added as they come in. If an initial evaluation showed some dissatisfaction with the workings of the building, a follow-up a year or two later might show that the occupants had learned to use the building properly and that their degree of satisfaction with it had increased proportionately. The present informa-tion system in architecture is based on one-shot and highly subjective ap-praisals. No information or evaluation system can be infallible, but at least it can correct mistakes or premature conclusions once they are recognized.

2. Retrieval capacity should be rapid and decentralized. A designer in a small city should have access to a common open-ended information pool.

3. The evaluation must include behavioral as well as technical data. It must be more than a collection of plans or blueprints.

4. Categories should be clearly specified, not only to aid people seek-ing information, but to guide evaluations. Technical jargon should not interfere with intelligibility. Most articles on noise use decibels as the meas-uring unit. This is fine except that decibels are logarithmic which produces all sorts of interesting arithmetic anomalies. If you take a 60 decibel noise and add another 60 decibel noise to it, the result is a sound that comes out to 63 decibels. There is a great deal of propaganda about the supersonic transport which, at 1500 feet, will produce a noise level of only 12 decibels over that of a DC3 at the same altitude (an increase from 110 to 122 decibels). The government reports do not mention that a 12 decibel rise is not an increase of only one tenth, but an increase of *four times* the 110 decibel noise level of the DC3. Would a homeowner really object if the sound level from a new freeway increases only 4 or 5 decibels? Unfortu-nately he may find that an increase of this amount of a given noise could double noise intensity.[9] A decibel system for measuring noise should cer-tainly be supplemented by another system that deals with units of subjec-tive intensity or discomfort using an arithmetic scale. From a psychological standpoint, logarithmic measurement works in a similar manner to an adap-tation process—the more intense a stimulus, the more change it takes to be noticed as a difference. One must be exceedingly wary of the units which

[9]D. Hall, "Noise Just Doesn't Add Up Like It Used To," *Daily Californian*, April 27, 1970, p. 2.

use the existing level of the problem as a baseline. This has the built-in tendency to encourage the reader to accept the existing level of the problem.

5. There should be a minimum of *ad hominem* statements. One is looking at environmental systems rather than at the people who built them. Evaluation is not a ponderous awards system that includes booby prizes as well as blue ribbons; it involves the objective assessment of buildings, parks, or components, according to specified criteria. These criteria include initial cost, maintenance, aesthetic appeal, comfort, and others. The design enterprise depends upon people and the adequacy of design will depend in large measure upon the creativity and sensitivity of designers, but the evaluation of a structure must deal with the product rather than the creator.

Evaluation as a Teaching Tool

What is the likelihood that a massive data bank on physical facilities will lead to a dreary sameness and regimentation? To what extent will norms become codes, to become buildings, to become obstacles to change? Frankly I don't have any ready answers. When people have learned what makes a good children's playground and have made this information available, what incentive will there be for a town council or school board to experiment with a new sort of playground? The answer must lie with man's creative capacities—his desires to innovate, build, personalize, and put his imprint upon the world around him. My hope is that designers, who have access to a data bank of playgrounds and who don't have to invent each piece of equipment that they use or to draw upon bad stereotypes of good playgrounds, will have more time to examine the unique characteristics of the site, neighborhood, and play habits of local youngsters. The data bank could provide the basis for descriptive booklets, brochures, and films. If people in the neighborhood cannot visit an adventure playground, at least they can see a film showing how it is being used, read what other parents and children think about it, and study the problems connected with maintenance or security.

I also believe that evaluations are humanizing since they sensitize people to their environment. Several qualifications are obviously in order. First, we have to assume that the questions deal with topics that have some meaning and relevance to the respondents. Questions about foreign aid or the British Labor Party don't have much meaning to most people in San Francisco. However asking a person about his own home, office, or neighborhood is humanizing because it makes him more aware of things around him. The second qualification is that the questions are asked in good faith. The people undertaking the survey must want to know the respondent's needs and will put the information to use themselves, make it public, or will turn it over to those who can use it. There are numerous instances of surveys being used to delay action. Instead of referring a question to a committee, which used to be a way of stalling legislation, a city council may now recommend a survey. I am endorsing surveys as precursors to action rather than as substitutes. The third qualification is that at least some of the questions should allow the respondent a free range of answers. He should not be so constrained within predetermined categories that his answers will distort his real opinions.

When surveys are properly used there is an important tie-in between them and environmental awareness. A good survey is able to make people more aware of the issues about which they are being questioned. It can be an important tool in humanizing a drab institutional environment. David Vail, a creative psychiatrist who heads Minnesota's mental hospitals, uses a "ward living conditions questionnaire" which is filled out by hospital nurses on a ward-by-ward basis each year.[10] The questions are ingenuous and effective. Here are a few items:

3. Does the ward have a bulletin board easily accessible to view by all patients?

4. Is there a large calendar easily accessible to view by all patients?

6. Is there a piano in the ward?
   a. Has it been tuned in the last year?
   b. Is the piano used by patients?

8. Do the patients have access to a plot in which to grow a garden or flowers?
   a. Do they use it?

15. How many patients may watch TV after the 10 P.M. news?

16. How many patients may watch the midnight show?

I have always believed there is value in naive questions. Why aren't there live flowers in school buildings? Or in prisons? One reason may be that the question is never asked. Most surveys are like school examinations —they are designed for machine scoring and fixed categories of answers. A good survey like a good examination makes people think, it challenges their ideas, and shows how apparently disparate items can be related. There is no better way to get a community involved in preserving an historic building than to begin with an inventory of the area—what is there, how it is being managed and used, and what role it plays in the cultural, educational, and recreational life of the community. Those involved in undertaking the

---

[10]David Vail, *Dehumanization and the Institutional Career.* Springfield: Charles C Thomas, 1966.

survey often become the strongest proponents of action programs. High school students who undertake a survey of recreational opportunities for the elderly may be motivated to develop a volunteer visiting program. If they see how the local riverbank has become the dumping ground for local industries they may be moved to clean it up and to lobby for stricter controls over dumping. Frequently the reports issued by a survey team have less long-range significance than the educational value of the survey for the participants. There is generally a ripple effect from one program to another. When one building in an historical neighborhood is restored, it shows what can be done and forces people to look at neighboring buildings and ask why these cannot be restored also.

CHAPTER TEN

The New Evaluator Cookbook

The knowledge of the house is not limited to the builder alone. The user or master of the house will even be a better judge than the builder, just as the pilot will judge better of a rudder than the carpenter, and the guest will judge better of a feast than the cook.—ARISTOTLE

Anyone who wants only the general approach of the book can skip this chapter. It is concerned with the nitty-gritty of evaluation—how to do it. Keep reading only if you plan to perform evaluations yourself. This is a cookbook rather than a theory of food preference—designers are often advised to go back and evaluate their work, but no one tells them how it is done. The tools of the behavioral sciences are not that complicated (or shouldn't be in any event—most of the complicated ones aren't worth much). The actual interview forms, questionnaires, and observation sheets used in published research are generally difficult to obtain and are only available by writing to the individual investigator and asking for his original report.

Let me begin by presenting some instruments that have been used to evaluate buildings. As I have indicated elsewhere,[1] there is no single *best* method for gaining user-inputs; the methods should flow naturally from the problem and circumstances. Ideally one uses several different techniques and lets the evaluations extend over a period of time. The questionnaire is an excellent instrument when the respondents are college students but unsatisfactory when they are children or migrant farm workers. A simulation procedure, such as the bomb shelter described in Case E, may be worth trying providing the cost is not prohibitive.

[1] Robert Sommer, *Personal Space*. Englewood Cliffs, N.J.: Prentice-Hall, 1969.

Only partial illustrations of the various methods will be presented, but they should convey the goals and the methods of the investigator. These studies were made by designers, space managers, and social scientists. There are few available environmental surveys undertaken by consumer groups. At this time it seems to be left up to either designers or social scientists to generate user-inputs. Hopefully this situation will change.

CASE A

INTERVIEW: FORMER PATIENTS AT THE ROYAL VICTORIA HOSPITAL, BELFAST[2]

---

1. Physical conditions of hospital.
   (a) Size of ward. If you were planning a new hospital would you make the ward the same size as the one you were in or would you design it bigger or smaller?

   Have you anything you would like to comment on about—
   (b) The bathrooms
   (c) Ventilation and heating of the wards
   (d) Lighting
   (e) Beds and bedclothes

Comment. The interviews were conducted in the homes of former hospital patients by a trained interviewer. The 150 patients interviewed were a random sample selected from all 3,701 patients discharged from the Royal Victoria Hospital during a prescribed period. The questions were open-ended and later coded into categories by the interviewer. Open-ended questions are recommended in an exploratory survey such as this, and they are also desirable with respondents from a wide variety of backgrounds who will interpret questions differently. The survey helped the authors make specific recommendations to the hospital authorities, e.g., "Better temperature control of the wards appears to be necessary, particularly to avoid overheating; consideration should be given to the provision of more comfortable waterproof undersheeting, and attempts should be made to reduce noise in the main corridor at night." This is a good example of a small-scale economical survey dealing with a specific building and aimed at a finite population.

[2]M. Y. Dudgeon and T. W. Davidson, *Some Reactions of Patients to Their Stay in Hospital.* Institute of Clinical Science, University of Belfast, mimeographed report, 1965.

CASE B

LARGE-SCALE SURVEY: OFFICE BUILDINGS[3]

12. Is there any noise in this office from machines (other than typewriters) being used in other offices?

Yes	226
No	2017
N.A.	47

13. If you find it drafty at all in the office, summer or winter, where in the room do you feel it? Check one or more as applicable:

Throughout room	155
Near windows	603
Near doors	278
Along the floor	334
Cannot really say	201
N.A.	1108

16. Check any of the following statements that apply to your office:

Ventilation is in general satisfactory	1673
There are not enough windows for ventilation in summer	106
The windows can't be opened because of drafts, noise, dirt, or rain coming in	640
N.A.	119

17. Is there anything else you would like to say about the ventilation? Answer below.

Comment. This questionnaire was used in a large scale survey of almost three thousand London offices, built after 1945. The study was undertaken by the Building Research Station of the Ministry of Technology to learn overall satisfaction (or lack of it) with new office buildings. The scope of the investigation permits discussion of a building type in the most general sense and the conclusions would be most useful in governmental planning of new structures. However, the questionnaire can also be used by the management of individual offices to assay their own quarters.

[3]F. J. Langdon, *Modern Offices: A User Survey*, National Building Studies Research Paper 41. London: HMSO, 1966.

CASE C

SPECIFIC SMALL-SCALE SURVEY: BANK[4]

Part 1. Customer and Public Areas	EXCELLENT	GOOD	SATISFACTORY	NEEDS IMPROVEMENT	SUGGESTIONS
Lighting					
Temperature					
Building location					
Room sizes					
Ceiling heights					
Colors					
Furniture					
Atmosphere					
Check desks					
Tellers' counter					
Offices					
Director's room					
Quietness					
Pleasantness					
Customers' room					
Coffee room					

[4]Walter Duson, unpublished study, 1969.

Fountain					
Sign					
Parking					
Planting					
Location of drive-ins					
Location of night deposit					
Image to public					

Comment. This was part of a survey undertaken by the architects who designed the bank building. There are separate forms for each room in the bank; these are filled out only by people concerned with that area. Customers are asked about their own areas as well as the exterior aspects of the building.

Case D

Expert Ratings: Primary Schools[5]

Consider:

1. *Thermal comfort of the interior*
   Air temperature   measured values
   Experience of radiation (e.g., ceiling heating, sunlight,
       radiation heat loss to windows and cold surfaces)   measured values
   Temperature gradient (e.g., cold feet, hot head)
   Air freshness/stuffiness
   Air movement: stagnation, drafts   measured values
   Humidity   measured values
   Consistency-variability of thermal conditions
   Any aesthetic effects of thermal design?

2. *Thermal environmental design*
   Thermal properties of the building:
       heavy/light construction
       opportunities for solar penetration

[5]Peter Manning, ed., *The Primary School: An Environment for Education.* Department of Building Science, University of Liverpool, 1967.

thermal insulation
treatment of surfaces: inside, outside

Comment. Teams consisting of teachers, engineers, psychologists, and architects visited 20 primary schools in England and rated various dimensions of the environment—visual, thermal, aural, etc. The above questionnaire requires ratings for both measured values of temperature, air movement, humidity, and radiation as well as narrative description of the thermal environment. In this particular survey no effort was made to obtain ratings from teachers and pupils in the buildings.

CASE E

SIMULATED ENVIRONMENT: CIVIL DEFENSE SHELTERS[6]

A controlled environment made it possible for the authorities to provide options to the shelter inhabitants and then monitor the outcome. The results were stated in terms of the actual behavior of the shelter inhabitants—

"A mean temperature of 74 degrees was acceptable to the majority of people during the first week's period. However, somewhat higher temperatures—74–76 degrees—were preferred during the second week.

"The subjects used most of the available lighting at some period during the day. The lighting was raised in steps beginning just before 0800 hours and reached a maximum (583 watts) at 0900 hours. . . .

"The frequency and duration of latrine use were recorded by the use of a micro switch activated by the latrine door. . . . The mean duration of latrine use was between 3.1 and 3.7 minutes. . . ."

Comment. Evaluation is based on the recorded behavior of the respondents rather than what they say. One assumes that the stimulus levels selected by the people will meet their needs. The concept of evaluation is not greatly relevant in this sort of situation where the people control their own environment. However the data can be exceedingly useful for other systems where, because of economic or other factors, the respondents cannot control their own environment.

[6]*Shelter Occupancy Studies at the University of Georgia 1962–63*, mimeographed report from Psychological Laboratories. Athens, Georgia: University of Georgia, 1963.

CASE F

EVALUATION BASED ON PERCEPTUAL VARIABLES: COURTROOM DESIGN[7]

Preliminary interviews with attorneys, judges, and jurors had suggested that many problems in existing courtrooms resulted from poor vision, hearing, and

[7]Sim van der Ryn, "An Analysis of Courtroom Design Criteria," *Judicature*, No. 42, 4, November, 1968, pp. 150–155.

movement. The researchers then proceeded to measure visual angles toward the witness stand from all parts of the room and also to measure acoustic efficiency. They proposed several alternative arrangements of the courtroom.

Comment. This is a good example of a "second stage" evaluation study. Prior interviewing had already established that seeing and hearing were important factors in courtroom adequacy; the author directly addressed himself to the task of arranging courtroom participants so that each one could see and hear the others in the room. Whether the innovative designs have similar or different problems is, of course, a problem for further investigation.

CASE G

OBSERVATIONAL METHODS: SEVERAL PARKS IN LOS ANGELES[8]

An architectural firm was given the job of deciding how to use a large corner site in Los Angeles which might not be developed for several years. After the possibility of a public plaza was suggested, the firm undertook observational studies of several parks and plazas in adjacent areas. Their methods were observational and statistical—looking and counting.

. . . During the morning and afternoon the Civic Center Mall is not used to any significant degree. During lunch period, there is moderate usage by people eating sack lunches, reading, or conversing with one or more friends. At the time of peak use, less than 25 per cent of the seating capacity of the plaza was occupied. . . .

The most obvious use of Pershing Square is seen in the seating areas. These are almost exclusively occupied by older men on a semipermanent basis; season ticket holders as it were. . . .

The grounds of the Los Angeles Public Library are well-landscaped with mature plantings, there are shaded walks and ample seating. Anyone seeking peace and quiet in the center of a bustling city could find it on the library grounds. In fact, it proved to be the least used of the public grounds we investigated. . . .

Comment. Although the methods used were strictly observational, they generated some interesting hypotheses about park use and suggested what makes a downtown plaza attractive to local residents. Some interviews with park residents and also with people not using the park would have clarified and enriched the findings.

[8]Deasy and Bolling Architects, *People in the Streets, People in the Parks,* 1967. This excellent report is available directly from the architectural firm of Deasy and Bolling in Los Angeles and deserves a wider audience than it has received. The informal distribution system illustrates some of the difficulties in making user-evaluations available to practitioners.

CASE H

SELF-SURVEY BY DORMITORY RESIDENTS

Background. On April 30, 1970, I was asked by a member of the student government at a nearby college to visit his institution and talk with students about college dormitories. Money would be available for renovating the dorms, and the student officer believed that I might be helpful in establishing priorities. I suggested that before my visit the students themselves might survey their dorms and find out if people were satisfied with present accommodations and where improvements seemed warranted. I offered to supply a questionnaire, and my caller agreed to adapt it to local conditions, have it duplicated, distributed, collected, and tabulated. I arranged to visit the campus on May 19, 1970. I wanted to give the students sufficient time for the survey and, at the same time, not let their interest wane. I arrived at the college in the afternoon, toured the dormitories accompanied by the student body president, and then went into hiding for a few hours to collect my wits and go over the survey replies. Incidentally, I toured the dorms *before* looking at the questionnaire replies, since I was afraid that the replies might bias my observations.

We visited one or two rooms on each floor of each dorm. The student body president was a good guide, although his presence may have inhibited some of the students. We talked informally with the occupants and asked them what they liked and disliked about the dorm, the relative advantages and disadvantages of living on campus, and other questions. We also noted what the students had done to their rooms—how they placed their beds, their use of posters, curtains, and wallcoverings, indications as to where they actually studied, etc. The students displayed a great deal of creativity in decorating and arranging their own rooms, but they lacked any real concern about public areas. The dorm lounges were barren and inhospitable—only one showed signs of human habitation, and that one had become the private preserve of an art student, who used it as his studio. The kitchenettes were dirty and lacked utensils, the craft room barren and lacking supplies. Noise was felt to be a serious problem by everyone. The questionnaire replies not only corroborated our observations but considerably extended them. The tabulation of the replies from 60 students is presented below.

How would you rate your present living accommodations with regard to each of the following?

	Excellent or Satisfactory	Needs Improvement
Living expenses	11	50
Quiet	13	49
Privacy	28	33
Informal social life	31	30
School spirit	31	25
Study arrangements	18	46
Organized activities	33	24

	Excellent or Satisfactory	Needs Improvement
Student government	39	21
University restrictions	35	26
Amount of living space	21	42
Housework (cleaning, etc.)	37	23
Faculty contacts	51	9
Dining or eating facilities	25	35
Laundry facilities	16	49
Parking facilities	27	34
Lounges	15	44
Bike racks	32	26
Closet space	36	31
Bookcases	15	47
Heating	11	54
Desks	43	19
Sports facilities	29	25
Furnishings	29	33
Soundproofing	3	58
Landscaping	39	20
Lighting (inside)	38	24
Lighting (outside)	52	8
Coed living	24	26
Air conditioning	6	48

4. Living where you do, do you feel isolated from the rest of the campus? Yes—34; No—20; Don't know—5.

5. Overall, considering everything, how do you rate your present living accommodations?   Excellent—1; Good—6; Fair—33; Poor—14; Terrible—7.

Household Hints

A good file of recipes and a knowledge of kitchen equipment are not enough to transform a housewife into a gourmet chef. There has to be talent and, above all, practice. I have no desire to turn designers into third-rate social scientists or social scientists into third-rate designers. However, I believe it is important to give architects and other environmentalists access to the tools and concepts of behavioral research so that they can talk and work with social scientists and, if they have the time, inclination, and talent, can conduct behavioral studies themselves. For a designer who wants to go further into research techniques, I would recommend several excellent works such as *Research Methods in Social Relations*[8] and Volume Two of

[8]Claire Sellitz, *et al.*, *Research Methods in Social Relations, Revised Ed*. New York: Dryden Press, 1959.

the *Handbook of Social Psychology*,[9] the chapter on participant observation by Becker and Geer,[10] the pamphlet by Burch[11] on observation in recreation research, as well as some of the actual studies that have been cited in this chapter.

Besides the individual recipes, let me offer several guidelines that will help a person to do a better job in evaluation. At least they will help him avoid mistakes that other investigators have made.

Avoid asking people to rate "offices in general" or "classrooms in general." There are good and poor classrooms and good and poor offices as well as mediocre ones. Such "general evaluations" are based on stereotypes and on composite concepts that may have very little specific relevance. It is better to ask a secretary about her own office or a teacher about her own classroom.

Observations should precede interviews. In a new setting, particularly, one should not ask questions until one knows what to ask about. Even on familiar turf it is wise to watch the action for a few hours before beginning formal interviews. In an interview, one may hear a lot but one is not likely to see much. The general rule is to begin with less obtrusive procedures before using those likely to change the attitudes and behaviors of the people involved. One may find that a hallway between two apartments is the nexus of conversations or that the phone on one person's desk rings continually and annoys other people in the office. This information can be gleaned from interviews providing one asks the right questions. But some observations beforehand, with a minimum of preconceptions, are usually a good investment.

One must sample *uses* as well as *users*. A library may be suitable for reference scholars yet still be a poor place to study. A waiting area outside a main office may be very satisfactory with less than five occupants but be grossly uncomfortable when there are more than ten. In some classrooms we studied, for example, complaints about ventilation ranged from zero at low occupancy to 95 per cent at peak occupancy.

Avoid asking detailed questions first. It is preferable to begin with general questions—what do you like about this airport and what do you feel needs improvement? After this, one can ask questions about specific items. When one asks the specific questions first, the respondent is overwhelmed by the detailed material and is unlikely to come up with general impressions later.

[9] G. Lindzey, ed., *Handbook of Social Psychology, 2nd Ed.* Reading, Mass.: Addison-Wesley Publishing Company, Inc., 1969.

[10] H. S. Becker and Blanche Geer, "Participant Observation and Interviewing: A Comparison," *Human Organization*, No. 16 (1957), pp. 28–32.

[11] William R. Burch, Jr., *A New Look at an Old Friend—Observation As a Technique for Recreation Research*. Portland, Oregon: Pacific Northwest Forest and Range Experiment Station, 1964.

Avoid using words or phrases beyond the level of the respondent. The vocabulary level of many people is depressingly low. Words like "ornate" or "homogeneous" may confuse respondents. "Static" may suggest poor TV reception rather than lack of movement. Each profession, including architecture, has its own jargon.

Always pretest whatever questionnaire or interview form you propose to use. I cannot state this too strongly. There is no substitute for a pilot test—one simply cannot conceive of all possible contingencies. This means that one does *not* mimeograph the first version of a questionnaire or interview form. It is too easy to continue using it "because it is available" or because a certain number of respondents have already answered it. It is best to leave a first draft handwritten or typewritten to emphasize its provisional character.

How many people should be interviewed, how many items should be included on the questionnaire, and how long should observations last? These are all reasonable and important questions, but they have no absolute answers. One simply observes enough people for as long a time as is necessary to get a good picture of what they do; and one interviews enough people to have some confidence that he knows what they think. One tries to get representative groups where it is possible, but there is rarely the need for the precision required by public opinion pollsters.

Is it necessary to evaluate "all" aspects of a building? The answer is, of course, no, since there are always time and money limitations on a project. In a very practical sense one tries to evaluate as many relevant dimensions as one can within the time and resources available. If the evaluation is being done as part of a Ph.D. thesis, a man can invest a full year evaluating a building on a part-time basis. On the other hand, if the evaluation of an existing building is part of the programming for some new construction with a tight deadline, then the evaluations may have to take place over a two-day period. I should like to emphasize that part-time evaluation over a long period would probably prove less disruptive to a client's activities, and would distort the nature of those activities less, than a crash evaluation completed in a day or two. Particularly when observation is involved, it is important to let the people in the building become accustomed to the presence of the observer and allow them to act naturally when he is around.

Before concluding this section, I want to emphasize that this "loose" and pragmatic philosophy applies to actual field studies to be undertaken by people concerned with environmental problems. When the study is an academic effort, the criteria and the standards necessarily change. For the most part, I have avoided discussing techniques and tools that required extensive background in mathematics or statistics. I have focused on the evaluation methods which I believe have the most favorable cost-benefit ratio for the individual practitioner. As detailed data banks are developed, more sophisticated approaches to measurement and analysis will be required.

CHAPTER ELEVEN

Beyond Productivity

The western scientific achievement, great though it is, has not concerned itself enough with the creation of better human beings, nor with self-discipline. It has concentrated instead upon things, and assumed that the good life would follow.—LOREN EISELEY

In the decades since World War II, interest has shifted in turn from the physical sciences to psychology, to the fine arts, to the biological sciences, and now to ecology. Time has speeded up to such an extent that these intellectual currents sweep by in years rather than in decades as they used to. Another current, this one from philosophy, will have to join the stream in order to set some direction to the flow. Ecology and even architecture, without concepts of environmental quality, remain empty exercises. The adaptability of man has made it possible for him to live in the crowded and dirty New York City subways; the destruction of the green areas of the nation has become a feasible reality. The only solution is to deal with issues of value and quality—to discover how people want to live and to develop institutional means for realizing desired life styles. We must stop looking at experiences and objects solely in terms of what they mean for other things and see them for what they represent themselves.

There is a pervasive insensitivity to experience unless it can be labeled, wrapped, and marketed. The tourist sees the Grand Canyon through his camera, thinking of the way the slides will appear to his neighbors on the screen back home. His emotional energy is bound up with the fact that he is at the Grand Canyon, with comparing trailers and campgrounds, and with anticipating his imminent return trip. In order to emphasize his experience he does not need to reject material relationships or interdependencies, for these are the basis of natural law, but he needs to give validity to sense impressions too. We tend to tune out reality in favor of empty abstractions. Ugliness and congestion mean ugliness and congestion as well as population growth and urbanism.

Ten years ago I believed the question was Adaptation, yes, but at what cost? and that I would attempt to measure the cost in individual and social pathology. Unfortunately the complexity of modern life combined with the adaptive capacity of man made this approach virtually unusable. There is simply no way to "prove" that a dirty, poorly-lit, or crowded school will increase juvenile delinquency or mental illness. The implications of this statement are not as frightening or anti-intellectual as they sound; it took a long time before I was able to penetrate my own jargon. Although these effects cannot be proven by absolute scientific standards, one *knows* that poor schools don't do children any good and will probably do them some harm. One reason why this obvious fact cannot be proved is that poor schools simply don't exist "by themselves"; they accompany rundown neighborhoods with high crime rates, unemployment, alcoholism, and virtually every other form of social pathology. There is no way apart from creating some highly esoteric and artificial experiment—which would be extremely costly, time consuming, and would almost certainly end up with ambiguous results—to establish something that doesn't have to be proven in the first place. This is not a retreat to mysticism, but rather an explicit statement that the quality of life is a matter of human values and cannot be established by scientific proof. We must decide how we want to live and then use our supertechnology to achieve those ends.

At the moment the trend is to evaluate buildings, neighborhoods, and cities using external productivity standards. This is in accord with Western notions of instrumental value—X is valuable because it leads to G which is valuable because it leads to M. There is no end to this chase after instrumental value, no end except the 72 years allotted to each of us. This is part of the frontier myth which forever points somewhere beyond, and does not square with the fact that space on this earth is finite. *We have arrived and we had better find out where we are.* We can no longer view individual acts or social programs solely on the basis of their implications for other acts or programs. We must begin to accept the nature of the act itself as the basis for evaluation.

Perhaps my argument will be clearer after one or two examples. Lady Allen of Hurtwood[1] pioneered the adventure playground which lets children play with all sorts of junk. How does one evaluate the effects of an adventure playground on children? I regard the question as a semantic

[1]Lady Allen of Hurtwood, *Planning for Play*. Cambridge, Mass.: The M.I.T. Press, 1969.

trap, but let me answer it anyway. The typical approach of the social scientist would be to develop "tests" which could be used to compare children in conventional playgrounds with children in adventure playgrounds. The tests would measure physical fitness, muscular coordination, and creative thinking ("How many uses can you find for a tin can?"). The evaluator might also check to see if vandalism and the incidence of childhood neurosis were lower in neighborhoods with adventure playgrounds. Until a few years ago, this was my own approach to this sort of problem. I am still sympathetic to the intent behind it, but I have learned through repeated experience that it is a blind alley. People are extraordinarily resilient; it is highly unlikely that one can "prove" by traditional scientific standards that the adventure playground builds physical fitness or muscular coordination or strengthens creative thinking more than any other sort of playground. Yet by observing the children in an adventure playground, one sees immediately that they are more active, happier, and more cooperative in their play, and more inventive in their range of activities. It is indeed frustrating to be unable to demonstrate this difference in subsequent activities or measurements.

Some years ago the common sense approach to adventure playgrounds would have involved the free operation of market mechanisms—build two playgrounds side by side, one adventure and one structured, and see which one the kids use. Perhaps it is because we live in a culture dominated by experts that there is now a great distrust of any evaluation based on free choice. One must now prove that the kids in adventure playgrounds behave better or produce more in some other context—at home, in school, or on some standardized test. A true scientific experiment requires that the children be arbitrarily placed in one playground or another. The same logic pervades the evaluation of Head Start and other enrichment programs. It does not seem to be enough to show that children will attend these if they are available, and will draw, read, and write. To justify these programs, one must demonstrate superior performance by the child after he has left the program.

The same arguments apply to the preservation and the restoration of historical buildings. There is no way to prove that the preservation of a row of trees or brownstone houses or the Imperial Hotel will lower the incidence of mental illness, reduce divorce rate, or increase national income. There is no point in trying to prove any of these things because they will obviously not occur. It seems more reasonable and honest to say that we appreciate their historical, cultural, and educational value. We can back this up with research into the roles that historical buildings play in the life of a community—how many people visit these buildings and the sorts of experiences they have, including feelings of continuity and a sense of the past. Just as the Department of Interior is presently encouraging schools to use parks as ecological preserves, restored buildings can also greatly enrich courses in history and social studies. History is often taught without

Collecting and crushing tin cans is one way to develop environmental awareness. It is too early to say whether community recycling campaigns represent a real step away from the frantic production-consumption cycle and toward a more balanced relationship with nature.

any personal or even community relevance for the child; it is a matter of memorizing arbitrary dates of remote events in faraway places. Almost any community is a laboratory of time-worlds. Preserved and restored buildings —including covered bridges, ice houses, and turn-of-the-century factories —are as important in maintaining our cultural heritage, as the preservation of wildlife ranges and forests is in maintaining contact with our biological heritage. When someone listens to a concert, attends a good play, or views a great work of art, is it legitimate to measure this in terms of its effect upon his marriage or his job or his IQ? It seems enough that he has had a good experience and that he feels that he derived something from it even if we cannot measure this change by productivity criteria. It is illogical to evaluate the open-plan school in terms of the number of graduates admitted to college or by their scores on college board exams. One is not likely to find much of a difference or improvement. On the other hand, these students won't perform any worse on exams, either. If this is the case, and I believe it is, one must turn to other methods for deciding the value of new social programs or innovative buildings. In our thinking about environmental problems, some form of bill of rights is necessary. This would include provision for adequate food, shelter, medical services, and recreational space. It should not be necessary to prove the correctness of one axiom on the basis of another. That is, one should not have to prove that a person needs good housing because it will affect his health or his education or his income.

At one of our workshops for developing environmental awareness, a hospital administrator asked if there were studies showing that patients would recover more rapidly if they knew what was going to happen to them and the reasons why things were done. Certainly the question was well-intentioned and reasonable. I would have liked to give him a direct affirmative answer. Life would be much easier if every improvement in a physical or social environment produced a clear and measurable increase in human health, creativity, and productivity. I am afraid that there is simply no way to establish a one-to-one connection between informed hospital patients and recovery time. Instead we have to use common sense and be clear about our own values. It should be obvious that the comfort of a hospital patient is a goal in itself—without reference to productivity, profit, or even physical health. If a patient feels more relaxed when he knows where a nurse is taking him and what is going to happen in the X-ray room, that should be reason enough to keep him informed.

A description of Mexico's Tres Marias Penal Colony, which provides an extraordinary amount of personal freedom for its inmates, concluded on a similar note.[2] After stating that any correctional institution must

---

[2]Donald P. Jewell, "Mexico's Tres Marias Penal Colony," *Journal of Criminal Law, Criminology and Police Science,* No. 48 (1957), pp. 410–413.

ultimately be judged by the degree to which its released inmates avoid further crimes, the author concedes that this is, at least for the present, an unrealistic and unfair criterion. Instead he recommends "that evaluation must be made in a more subjective manner, based on what is being done with what is available" and in this regard "there is little doubt that Tres Marias is demonstrating outstanding resourcefulness, ingenuity, and originality." I believe that if Tres Marias provides personal freedom and opportunities for education and vocational skills, then it is a far better prison than most in this country.

Values Rather Than Needs

A recent article on recreational planning stated that there is no compelling evidence that a lack of recreation leads to physical or social ills within our society.[3] This statement is true, of course, if one uses the physical scientist's concept of evidence. On the other hand, it is obvious that a large number of people, probably most people, want available outdoor recreational facilities. Implied in the concept of "need" is the idea that there is a biological basis for the behavior, and furthermore that frustration of the "need" will produce observable biological damage. To speak of "wants" or "values" avoids this pitfall. I hesitate to play word games, but it seems preferable to discuss human values (what people believe is good) and human wants (what people desire) rather than need with its implication of biological deficit. The justification for satisfying "needs" is that negative social behaviors produced by their frustration will be avoided. However the subjectivity of needs makes this a blind alley. Let me use what might be an obvious example—I hope to demonstrate it is not obvious at all— the belief that prison inmates need well-prepared food. If one uses the ground rules of the recreation specialist or the physical scientist, there is no "proof" that cold or unappetizing dinners cause prison riots or interfere with rehabilitation. Even when prisoners who have rioted include good food in their list of demands, everyone involved is quick to supply 10 other reasons for the disturbance. The same was true of the turmoil at universities following the Free Speech Movement at Berkeley in 1964. The immediate issue was the right of students to engage in political activity on campus, but the disturbance was blamed on a multitude of other factors, including an overemphasis on research, the ponderous size of the institution, the detachment of the administration from the day-to-day affairs of the campus, the increased political consciousness of the students who had

[3]S. G. Styles, "The Recreation Planning Process," *Proceedings of the 1969 Park and Recreation Administrators Institute*, Davis, California: University of California Extension, 1970.

participated in the Mississippi project the previous summer, the irrelevance of traditional curricula, the development of a nonstudent culture on Telegraph Avenue, and other reasons. One cannot "prove" that any of these factors produced the turmoil and its aftermath. When considering complex social behavior it is naive to expect a one-to-one connection between two events separated in space-time. One can state clearly that the Berkeley students *wanted* to participate in university decision-making, resented the overemphasis on research, and believed that the university administration was uninterested in them. Indeed, one can document these beliefs in an objective manner using the techniques of the public opinion pollster. Interviewing prison inmates, one quickly learns that they *want* well-prepared meals. Whether they *need* well-prepared meals seems an irrelevant question, if need implies a deep-seated biological drive with measurable consequences following frustration.

I hope it is clear that I am not rejecting the idea of needs, either biological or sociological. There is ample evidence, and hard evidence by anyone's standards, that rats and monkeys and people have a need for a varied stimulus environment; if this is frustrated during early years, they will be intellectually and emotionally impaired. However, one cannot relate these experiments to the desires of the residents of downtown Philadelphia for another park. It seems bad strategy to promote good environmental experiences for city dwellers on the basis of experiments with crowded rat cages or isolation chambers. Although this may be a successful tactic in the short run, it will eventually bring the environmental movement into disrepute. The solution is not to twist the methods of science, or to ignore them, but to use them in the service of humane values. Good experiences should be made an end in themselves—visitors to an art museum should experience beauty and delight, and people in a park should be able to commune with nature and have breathing space amidst urban congestion. The methods of science can be used to determine the connection between design elements and human responses.

Thus far we have argued strenuously against an exclusive reliance on productivity criteria in deciding environmental issues. It would probably be helpful if we faced the question, When *do* productivity standards apply? The answer, it seems to me, is that productivity standards are valid when all inputs and outputs can be stated in some quantitative form, and when a causal relationship exists between them. Unfortunately this doesn't ever seem to apply to pressing social issues. There is always a weighing of alternatives in which gains and losses cannot be assigned equivalent scores. One cannot seek values as if they are something out there to find. Man *creates* values; he can assign any value he chooses to a wild river valley, a minipark, or a whooping crane. Eventually the problem becomes a political one and must be settled on political terms.

Productivity standards have more relevance for producers than for consumers. A consumer doesn't particularly care that General Motors has doubled its production over the past 20 years or that visitors to national parks increase by a certain percentage annually. When he wants to visit a park himself, he probably would prefer fewer people there and he wants the highways to be a little less crowded than they are now. Consumers have an indirect stake in such productivity measures as employment rates or income levels but their particular interests do not coincide with those of producers. It is the responsibility of government to see that the legitimate interests of both producers and consumers are adequately represented. It is not enough to emphasize producer values—gross national product, number of automobiles produced, or airline miles traveled. Direct relevance for the consumer consists in his satisfaction with the product or service, and with the quality of life as well as the quantity of things.

We are arguing for proximate or short-range experiential criteria. Interestingly enough, the most hard-nosed group of psychologists—the Skinner-type behaviorists—use the same argument. Teodoro Ayllon[4] developed methods for motivating chronic mental patients to feed and clothe themselves and to take care of their rooms. While his critics charge that this amounts to adjusting the patient to the hospital routine without guaranteeing that his "mental health" is improved, Ayllon replies that his objective is behavior change *per se*. Whether this change is related to earlier discharge from the hospital or with the patient's improvement on psychological tests are other matters. The same goals apply to those behavior therapists who work with problems of individual clients on an outpatient basis. Someone who is afraid of heights or exposed places might be given desensitization therapy for his particular fears. Whereas the psychoanalyst complains that this deals with the "symptom" rather than with the patient's "real problem," the behavior therapist replies that the behavior *is* the problem for which the patient requested treatment. This is really the same argument that we have been using about the value of experiences in parks and buildings and schools. It should be enough to demonstrate that people enjoy themselves in a park, feel some communion with growing things and the outdoors, and have the opportunity to relax and socialize away from smog and crowds. It is not incumbent to demonstrate that this is related to anything else. We are not advocating a total immersion in subjectivity; the proximate criteria of the success of the program can be clearly and objectively stated. In fact they are more capable of clear and objective statement than the remote criteria of mental health and social adjustment in which innumerable other factors cloud the picture.

[4]Teodoro Ayllon and N. Azrin, *The Token Economy*. New York: Appleton-Century-Crofts, 1968.

A Language of Spatial Experience

Architecture generally affects people beyond the focus of awareness. Even when attention is focused directly on a building, people are concerned mainly with its shell, exterior, and the partitions. They are seemingly unaware of the qualities of interior space. The visitor uses dimensions of extensity and duration—the size of the area and how long he remained—and perhaps his affective response to the building. However, as Philip Thiel[5] reminds us, if music were limited to these same dimensions—the number of pieces played and the length of time the audience remained at the concert—or how people responded to the concert as measured by some seven-point rating scale—we would know very little about the nature of musical experience. Thiel describes a new social role called *envirotecture* which is concerned with the process of continuous environmental experience. The envirotect does not design furnishings, vehicles, rooms, buildings, cities, or highways—he designs potential experiences in any or all combinations of these parts of the environment. His chief tool is the sequence notation system or score (similar to a musical notation system) with which he describes a proposed or existing sequential system. Kevin Lynch[6] has developed a spatial notation system for city images, Donald Appleyard[7] has designed one for highways, and Lawrence Halprin[8] a "motation" system for landscape experience. Thiel argues cogently that without an informed, sensitive, alert, and critical audience able to communicate responses, the performance of the environmental manager is largely unchallenged. Discipline and art languish when there is a preoccupation with peripheral and irrelevant activities, and remedies take the form of cosmetic palliatives. With its refrains that "getting there is half the fun" and "it's not how long you make it, it's how you make it long," Madison Avenue has picked up the idea that experience itself is important, providing, of course, that one is spending money at the same time. The task of the envirotect, the self-conscious designer of experiences, will be made much easier when he has a language to define, organize, and lay out people's environmental experiences. Such a language will aid us in going beyond the hyperactive production-consumption cycle. For the designer, this means helping people to get the most from their surroundings. The architect's job is not simply to build-them-up so that others tear-them-down, but to help people to use things better and to improve the quality of living.

[5]Philip Thiel, *Towards an Envirotecture*. Book manuscript in preparation.

[6]Kevin Lynch, *The Image of the City*. Cambridge: The Technology Press, 1960.

[7]Donald Appleyard, Kevin Lynch, and J. R. Meyer, *The View from the Road*. Cambridge, Mass.: M.I.T. Press, 1964.

[8]Lawrence Halprin, "Motation," *Progressive Architecture*, July, 1965.

CHAPTER TWELVE

The Politics of Design

I believe the loss of our tax exemption was a blessing for the Sierra Club. Our major battles are political and social, and we now wage them where the action is. Changing the American life-style is a more basic issue and will require continuous and sustained effort.—JUNE VIAVANT

Every design decision has political implications. Middle class home-owners are in favor of public housing—somewhere else. They believe there should be a place where teen-agers can obtain help for drug problems as long as it is located—somewhere else. A new factory in town will be good for business but it is going take over the last unused bit of river bank. A new city hall will help give the town a better image but it may not be worth those extra taxes. I am asked to help plan a neighborhood park in a suburban district, but I know the greatest need for parks is in the crowded downtown area. When a student undertakes a study of how buildings on his campus get built, he immediately is struck by the lobbying done by departments and administrative units for extra space, the bureaucratic arrangement of campus planning boards and state budget agencies, and even the political nature of the process by which the architect is selected and the plans are approved. Space is a valuable resource, and it is intimately connected with the prevailing power system. If one attempts to change the space allocations or the quality of space, there will be vibrations, not always sympathetic, within the power system.

Environmental policies take place in a system which has been characterized by decentralism, pluralism, bargaining, and coalition building. The result is that policy change is typically incremental, and what is feasible is only marginally different from existing policies since drastic measures

133

are in most cases outside the political pale.[1] I can image an ecology candidate running for the presidency on a platform calling for taxes on industry and agribusiness based on the amount they pollute the air and the water, removal of the tax subsidy for large families, controlled land prices and restricted developments around cities, a ban on the SST, the prohibition of private automobiles in downtown areas, and several planks related to war, racism, and sexism. It would be a fine platform and there would be considerable educational value if Paul Ehrlich or Ralph Nader ran on it. Considering the political realities and the ties of the media to industry, I would not be very hopeful of his being elected. However, the 1900 platform of the Socialist Party of the United States, once considered incredibly radical, is now a part of the gospel of both major parties. Eventually we may have a national environmental control center larger than the Pentagon (although a small center in Washington coordinating the activities of regional field offices in various parts of the United States and reporting to an international center in Paris, would be more in accord with ecological principles), but we are likely to move toward this gradually. This should not quiet the strident calls to action; without them the body politic might not stir at all. Although we are likely to grope our way toward environmental control rather than to march to the applause of multitudes on either side of the boulevard, the important thing is that we get there.

Environmental quality should not be measured by the intuitions and prejudices of a cadre of design professions, nor by a popularity contest among unenlightened masses, nor can it be tied to an absolute goal of productivity or efficiency. It is only meaningful in a context of informed and aware citizens who are able to choose among alternative life styles. In a totalitarian society, the leaders supply values for the inhabitants. In a democratic society, citizens work together to create values. The designer in the democratic society must educate the public to a higher level of environmental consciousness so that people can choose wisely, build creatively, and maintain the environment productively.

When I first began working with designers, I thought they wanted me to talk about aesthetics and perception. Were there tested empirical methods for learning what people wanted or thought was beautiful? How do people experience buildings? I am still concerned with these issues but they are usually less significant in determining how a building looks or where it is located than the political and economic system in which the building is planned, built, and used. It is not my goal to inhibit the artistic capabilities of the designer by introducing political considerations. For all

[1]R. O. Loveridge, *Socio-political Constraints on Establishing Policies for a Habitable Environment*. Paper given at the First National Symposium on Habitability, Los Angeles, May 11–14, 1970.

except a handful of master builders political considerations are already pre-eminent. If designers want to have an input into the significant questions of who builds what, where it is located, and how it is used—which are essentially political questions—they are going to have to enter the political arena. They will need allies, and the logical place to look for them is among the people who are likely to use the facilities.

Compared to a totalitarian state, American-style democracy is conservative in regard to social change. Change comes about slowly and incrementally. It may take decades for the effects of a Supreme Court decision or a new federal statute to be evident. Outcomes are frequently decided by the need to placate certain interest groups which have been overlooked previously and feel they have been wrongfully treated. When a wheel squeaks, it is likely to be oiled. My own efforts, and those of other social scientists in the environmental field, can be seen as a redress of the political balance which will add more weight to user-values and the quality of life and correspondingly less weight to productivity standards. The issues are complex indeed and there is no such thing as a final solution. Nature abhors the concept of balance; all is flux and change, growth and decline, the emergence of new forms and adaptations.

From the point of view of Washington, recycling represents a new major industry, but for the typical householder, it is the harbinger of a new life-style. It means learning to cook well and to enjoy meals rather than finish them hurriedly with a minimum of fuss and bother; maintaining the family car rather than trading it in; looking for new ways to use containers; and taking the same view toward human problems. There are profound political implications in the concept of a society dedicated to balance rather than to infinite and impossible expansion. It is not clear that our social institutions and political leaders are willing or able to respond to the pressures for ecological balance.

A new awareness of the interdependency between organisms and their environment is clearly evident among the young. If the solution were simply to wait until people over 40 were succeeded by their children, there would be considerable cause for optimism. Unfortunately social institutions also resist change. These institutions were originally created to maintain standards, provide service on a continuing basis, and insure the stability of society. They are by nature conservative and resistant to change. What we have recommended in the design fields as a continuous design-evaluation-redesign cycle also applies to social institutions. It will not be easy to develop environmental policies which are democratic in the most literal sense —environmental rules made by the people or their representatives—but the alternative is a totalitarian system. Considering the scope and nature of environmental problems, it seems evident that some organized political structures will have to make and enforce long-range decisions. The difference between a democratic and a totalitarian system will be the extent to which the governing boards are responsible to the people whose lives are affected by their decisions.

In the studio, a design problem can be considered in purely aesthetic and technical terms. It is both necessary and desirable that design students should be technically expert in siting, structures, and use of materials, as well as be sensitive to those qualities that make a building attractive, satisfying, and meaningful to its occupants. But outside of the studio it will be the political considerations, even more than technical and aesthetic ones, that determine what is built and where, who pays the cost, and how it will be used. Within very broad limits, we have the technology to construct whatever we want and place it wherever we choose, including on the moon. This is not to say that our resources are unlimited—far from it. Whatever we do, there will be a price tag attached to it. Design questions are all matters of deciding between alternative plans with different trade-offs. It is the task of the architect, the planner, and the environmental manager to know what those trade-offs are. As a professional, he has ethical obligations to the people who will actually use the facilities or be affected by them even though they are not technically his clients.

This is indeed a difficult task. To be hired, paid, and responsible to one group and attempt to satisfy the needs of another will inevitably produce conflicts in allegiance. A city housing board is likely to be more responsive to the wishes of real estate agents, banks, and suburban householders than to the needs of the urban poor. In the preceding chapters we spent considerable time discussing the difference between clients and users. I am *not* an advocate of the naïve notion that it is the designer's job to learn "the needs of the poor" by conducting surveys or by speaking to their representatives. Most of the time, the prospective users are not familiar with the options available and the various trade-offs involved in them. Rather than to take surveys dealing with hypothetical buildings, a far more practical approach is to evaluate structures already completed. Where a new prototype is involved, it should be tried on a small scale and use-tested thoroughly before it is mass produced. If a prototype is too expensive, it may be possible to build a housing project in stages, evaluating each part before additional units are constructed.

In the United States at least, the term *politics* has fallen on bad times. It generally appears in phrases such as *partisan politics, political boss,* or worst of all, *politician.* The origins of the word are much more benign. Both in Greek and Sanskrit, politics is identified with the state, the government, or form of administration. Hence acropolis is upper city, metropolis is mother city and cosmopolitan, a world citizen. The term refers to how people administer their own society, the sorts of rules established (policies), and the agents of administration (policemen and politicians). Questions concerning who is going to live where, who is going to pay the cost, whether or not there shall be government subsidies or tax write-offs, whether parks are developed in the cities or in the suburbs, are political in the fullest sense of the term.

A realization of this has come to virtually all the conservation organizations in the country. The Audubon Society has to combat policies which make oil spills inevitable, and the Wilderness Society must investigate tax policies that encourage speculative investments and phantom subdivisions in remote areas. Several years ago the Sierra Club, one of the most venerable of conservation organizations, lost its tax-exempt status in its battle to save the Grand Canyon from a power development project. Designers too must face up to the political implications of their work. I do not know how far one can generalize from the example of People's Park or other user-generated and user-maintained systems, but at least in theory they offer the promise of making life much simpler for the designer. His task is not to decide what people need but rather to help them realize their own goals. He is a technical expert in knowing the properties of materials, the laws of structure, the vicissitudes of climate and geography, but he has an equally important role in helping people make the most of what they build. There is economic justification for such a role, and a good architect can easily earn his per diem fee assisting people to live better. The planet cannot afford an architecture that is allied solely to the production-consumption cycle. Designers must break out of this cycle by becoming involved in the quality of life in existing buildings, towns, and cities.

Index